This book includes content that may be distressing to readers, including descriptions of discriminatory treatment of individuals, groups, religions or communities.

LADYBIRD BOOKS
UK | USA | Canada | Ireland | Australia
India | New Zealand | South Africa
Ladybird Books is part of the Penguin Random House group of companies whose addresses can be found at global.penguinrandomhouse.com.
www.penguin.co.uk www.puffin.co.uk www.ladybird.co.uk

First published 2024
001

Printed in China

The authorized representative in the EEA is Penguin Random House Ireland, Morrison Chambers, 32 Nassau Street, Dublin D02 YH68

A CIP catalogue record for this book is available from the British Library

ISBN: 978-0-241-57035-7

All correspondence to:
Ladybird Books
Penguin Random House Children's
One Embassy Gardens, 8 Viaduct Gardens
London SW11 7BW

MIX
Paper | Supporting responsible forestry
FSC® C018179

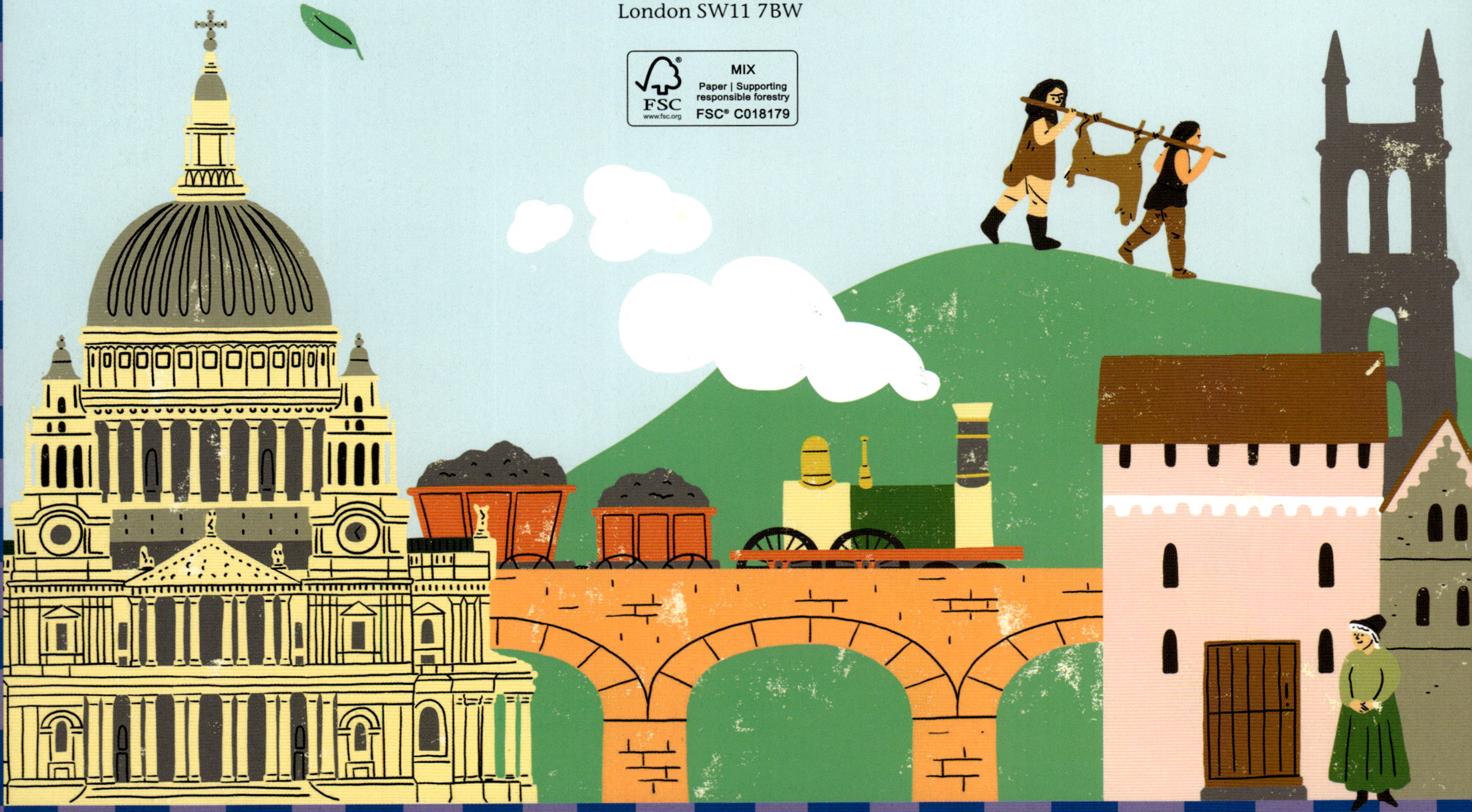

The BIG BOOK of UK HISTORY

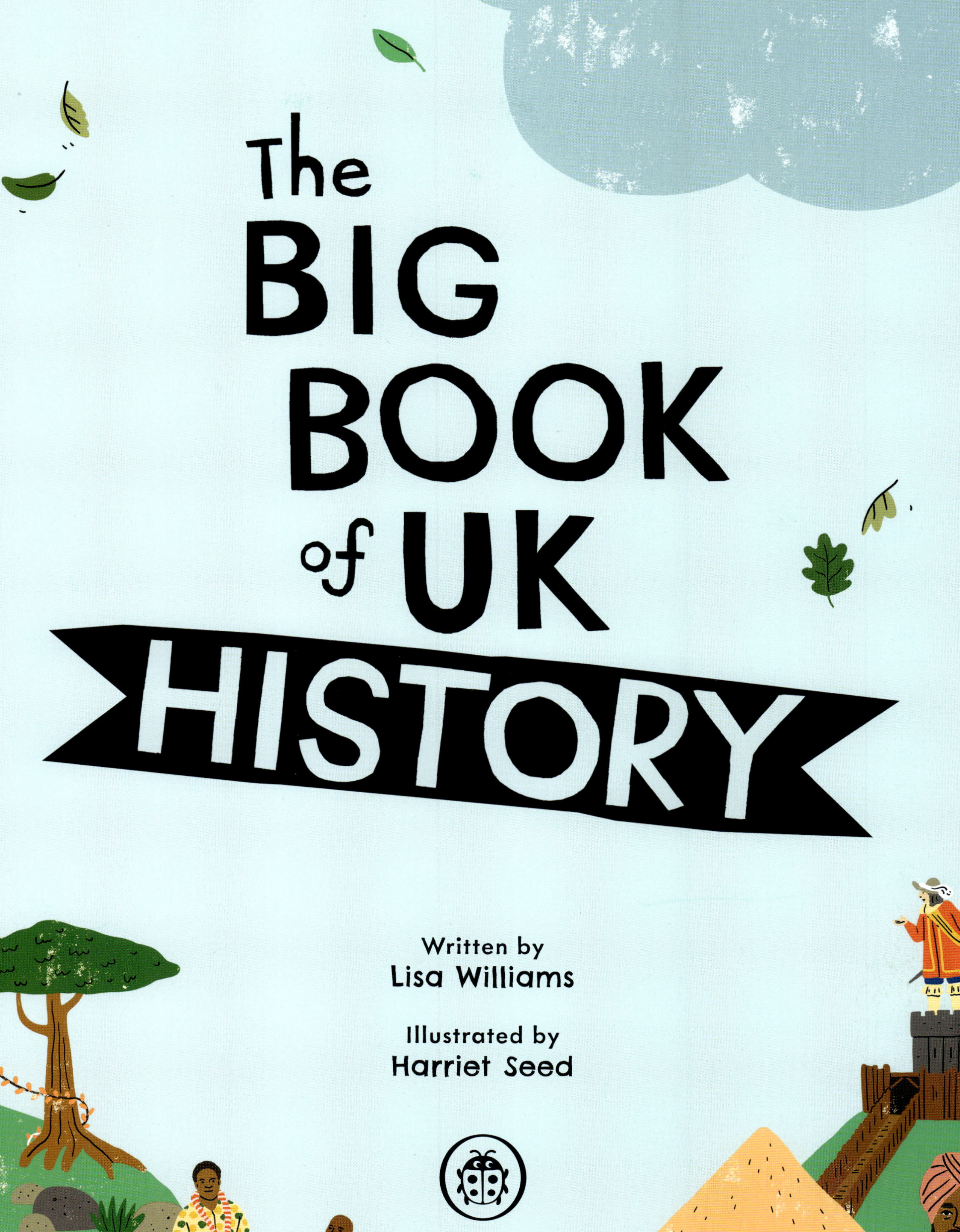

Written by
Lisa Williams

Illustrated by
Harriet Seed

Introduction

This book is **stuffed full** of amazing facts, taking you from **grisly plagues** and **grim witch trials** to great and glorious feats of **science, engineering** and **architecture**.

You'll discover who designed things, who built them and whose work provided the money to make it happen. As kings and queens battled for power in epic dramas, ordinary people fought their own battles for democracy and rights. You'll meet the brave people who demanded higher wages after the Black Death, those who fought against enslavement and the women who won the right to vote.

You'll learn how England, Wales, Scotland and Northern Ireland became the United Kingdom, and how each nation has held on to its cherished languages, traditions and identities. From the suffragettes to scientific discoveries, you'll learn about the people who have made our nation unique and vibrant.

Be inspired by the intriguing story of how this place came to be, and **discover** just how **exciting history can be!**

Contents

What is the United Kingdom?

The UK national flag is called the "Union Jack" or "Union Flag".

The United Kingdom of Great Britain and Northern Ireland (also known as "the United Kingdom" or "the UK") is an island nation in Western Europe in the North Atlantic Ocean. The United Kingdom includes the countries of England, Scotland, Wales and Northern Ireland.

"Great Britain" and "the United Kingdom" refer to different things. Great Britain is the name of the island where you'll find the countries England, Scotland and Wales. Northern Ireland is not part of Great Britain, but it is part of the United Kingdom.

The highest point in the UK is Ben Nevis in Scotland, which soars 1,343 metres above sea level.

SCOTLAND

NORTHERN IRELAND

Edinburgh

Belfast

The pound (£), the currency used in the UK, has existed for 1,200 years.

Roughly 68 million people live in the UK.

More than 300 languages are spoken in the UK.

Lough Neagh in Northern Ireland is the UK's largest lake, containing enough water to fill seven million swimming pools.

Wales has more castles per square mile than any other country in Europe.

IRELAND

WALES

ENGLAND

Cardiff

London

The countries in the UK have not always been united. At various points in history, they have been at war with one another. The current pact between the countries in the UK has existed since 1922.

This pact ensures that the UK is led by one democratic government and a monarchy.

London in England is the capital city of the UK. Roughly nine million people live here.

The land beneath your feet

To understand the United Kingdom's history, we must first understand how it came to be – literally! The surface of our planet is made from layers of rock that form our countries and continents. Over time, these layers of rock can slowly shift and drift, and in millions of years areas of land can move thousands of miles! Land can also collide and fuse together.

Pangaea

The surface of the Earth today looks dramatically different from when our planet was first formed. Originally, there were no seas. And, at one point, almost all the land was clumped together in one big mass called "Pangaea".

Now most of the land is broken up into seven big chunks – or "continents" – and spread across the globe. The UK is on the continent of Europe.

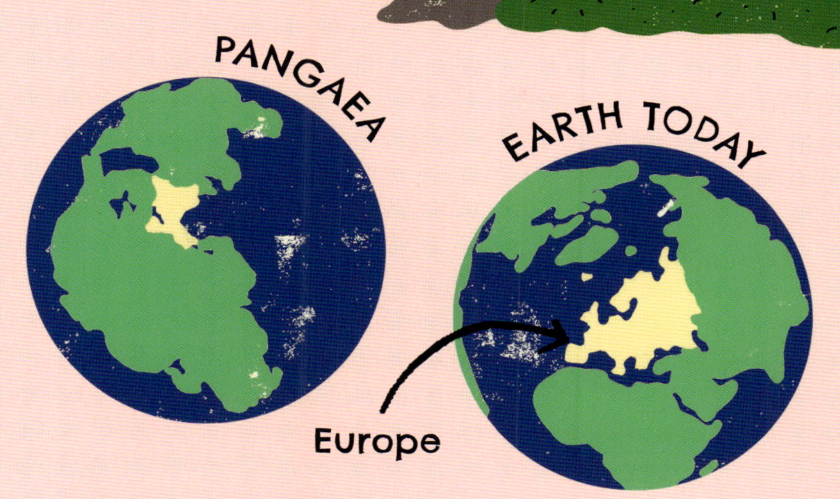

Regions of Scotland's north-west used to be connected to parts of Greenland and North America.

Believe it or not, the land of the United Kingdom was once in the southern hemisphere, near the South Pole! It moved north over millions of years. Now it's in the northern hemisphere, and it's steadily moving by roughly 2.5 centimetres each year.

The United Kingdom's oldest rocks can be found in Scotland. They are approximately 2.7 billion years old! Earth itself is 4.6 billion years old.

Prehistoric creatures

The UK was once home to dinosaurs and prehistoric creatures. Over 200 million years ago, monstrous marine reptiles and dinosaurs reigned over the seas and land.

The Jurassic Coast in Dorset, England, is one of the best places to find fossils in the United Kingdom.

Seas can rise and fall. More land appears when sea levels drop, and this can open up bridges to other countries and continents. The United Kingdom is now an island nation, but this wasn't always the case . . .

Early human evidence in the UK

The history of the UK starts with humankind. Roughly 950,000 years ago, the UK was connected to the rest of mainland Europe. South-west England was joined to northern France by a bridge of land, a chalk ridge known as the "Weald–Artois Anticline". Early human settlers walked along this bridge, forming small communities as they explored the UK.

950,000 years ago

The first humans in Britain were called "Britons".

The oldest evidence of humankind on UK soil dates from around 850,000 to 950,000 years ago.

These ancient footprints were found preserved in the mud in Happisburgh (*Haze-bruh*) in Norfolk, England.

Human tools dating back at least 700,000 years have been discovered at Happisburgh in Norfolk and Pakefield in Suffolk.

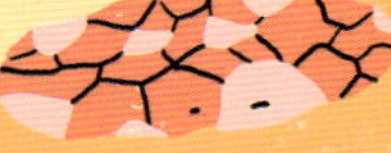

Two human teeth and a leg bone were discovered in Boxgrove, West Sussex. These older human remains date back 500,000 years.

In the distant past, hyenas, horses, mammoths and elk roamed wild in the UK. Life would've been tough for human settlers – the frozen landscape was harsh and food was scarce.

Archaeologists are scientists who study the history of humans by looking at objects that people left behind. Thanks to their work, we are constantly discovering more about humankind.

450,000 years ago

Our planet naturally warms and cools over periods of thousands of years, and roughly 450,000 years ago the temperature in the UK plunged. The climate became too cold for humans, and humankind disappeared from the island for thousands of years. The land bridge connecting England and the north of France was submerged during a catastrophic flood, known as a "megaflood". This created the beginnings of the English Channel, separating much of Britain from the continent.

400,000 years ago

Temperatures warmed once again, and humankind returned to UK soil using a narrow bridge of land. The 400,000-year-old skull of a young Neanderthal woman was discovered in Swanscombe, Kent.

The climate in Britain warmed and cooled over the next few hundred thousand years. When the UK was at its coldest, humankind could not survive, but at its warmest it welcomed new settlers.

Human species on UK soil

Homo antecessor

Homo antecessor was likely the first human species in the UK. Evidence suggests that Homo antecessor lived here at least 950,000 years ago.

Homo heidelbergensis

Homo heidelbergensis lived in the UK as early as 500,000 years ago. These people were skilled at crafting tools. They were excellent hunters, too – many remains of butchered animals, including horse, deer and woolly rhinoceros, have been linked to this time.

Homo neanderthalensis

Homo neanderthalensis, the "Neanderthals", lived in the UK at least 400,000 years ago. This species fled and returned to Britain many times until approximately 50,000 years ago, when they became extinct.

Homo sapiens

Homo sapiens (that's you!) is the only species of human still in existence. The earliest evidence of our species in Britain is a 40,000-year-old jawbone found in Devon, England. However, Homo sapiens appeared in Africa about 200,000 years ago.

Humankind came and went over the course of millennia. It is thought that from perhaps 180,000 years ago to 60,000 years ago, no human stepped foot on UK soil! Eventually, all but one species of human died out. Homo sapiens became dominant not just in the UK, but across the world . . .

Homo sapiens on UK soil

40,000 BCE

5,000 BCE

The earliest evidence of our species in the United Kingdom dates back 40,000 years. There have been many archaeological discoveries across these lands, and together they paint a vivid picture of what life may have been like for our ancestors.

Many of the earliest discoveries of humankind in the UK link to a period of time called the Stone Age. The Stone Age refers to the years in which early species of human, including our own species, Homo sapiens, used stone to make tools. The Stone Age is made up of three distinct periods. In the United Kingdom, they are:

The Palaeolithic Period, or Old Stone Age

During this time, humans began using basic stone tools. People were hunter-gatherers, which means they got food by hunting animals and gathering wild plants. They lived in small groups and travelled on foot to find food.

Mesolithic Period, or Middle Stone Age

When the Earth's climate cools for a long period, it is called an "ice age" or "glacial age". The Mesolithic Period followed on from the end of our planet's most recent ice age. As the glaciers melted, humans had to move around and adapt to the changing environment. People began polishing stone tools, and tools became more useful and complex.

Neolithic Period, or New Stone Age

During this period, many hunter-gatherers stopped their travels and stayed in one region. It marked the beginning of farming in many places around the world.

Cheddar Man

In 1903, a near-complete skeleton was unearthed in a cave in Cheddar Gorge, Somerset, England. The discovery of this 10,000-year-old skeleton, nicknamed "Cheddar Man", helped scientists understand what life may have been like for humankind all those years ago.

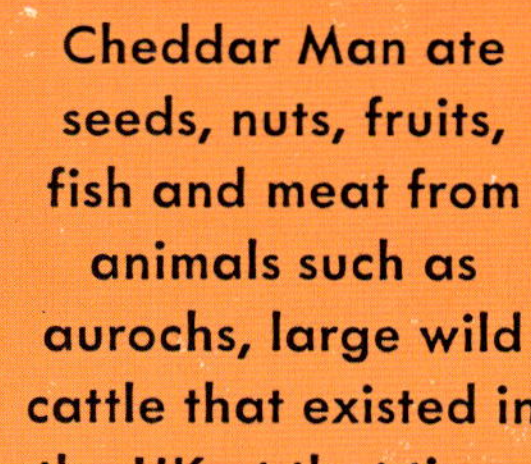

Cheddar Man ate seeds, nuts, fruits, fish and meat from animals such as aurochs, large wild cattle that existed in the UK at that time.

Cheddar Man's skeleton was so well preserved that scientists could conduct all sorts of tests. They learned that Cheddar Man had dark skin and pale blue eyes, and he was 166 centimetres tall.

Red Lady of Paviland

In late 1822, a band of geologists unearthed the remains of several mammoths in Goat's Hole Cave on the Gower Peninsula, Wales. A couple of months later, in January 1823, one of them discovered parts of a human skeleton, painted with red pigment.

The bones are thought to be at least 33,000 years old. The person was likely buried as part of some sort of ritual, making it one of the earliest documented burials in Europe.

The discoverers also found beads (just like you'd find on jewellery) and ornaments, so they believed they'd found the bones of a woman. However, the Red Lady of Paviland is actually the skeleton of a man!

Becoming an island

20,000 years ago, Britain was connected to Europe by a huge area of land known as "Doggerland". As the ice age ended and the ice began to melt in 10,000 BCE, sea levels started to rise, and Doggerland began to disappear. Then, 8,000 years ago, a tremendous landslide, called a "Storegga slide" was triggered near Norway creating a gigantic wave, called a "tsunami". This hurtled towards the UK, destroying everything in its path.

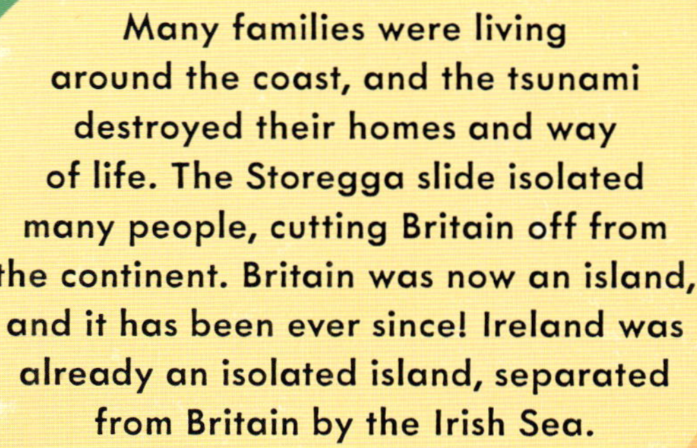

Many families were living around the coast, and the tsunami destroyed their homes and way of life. The Storegga slide isolated many people, cutting Britain off from the continent. Britain was now an island, and it has been ever since! Ireland was already an isolated island, separated from Britain by the Irish Sea.

Ancient sites

Stonehenge

Stonehenge on Salisbury Plain, England, is one of the most famous landmarks in the world. We're still not quite sure how this monument was built. Each of the enormous stones, called "sarsens", weighs roughly 25 tonnes, so moving the rocks and raising them off the ground would have required supernatural strength or a complex system of pulleys, ramps or tools, powered by hundreds of people.

A famous legend says that giants placed the original sarsens in Ireland and that a wizard by the name of Merlin magically transported them to England. In reality, archaeologists think people probably put the stones on huge sledges to shift them. Some of the stones came from as far as 139 miles away!

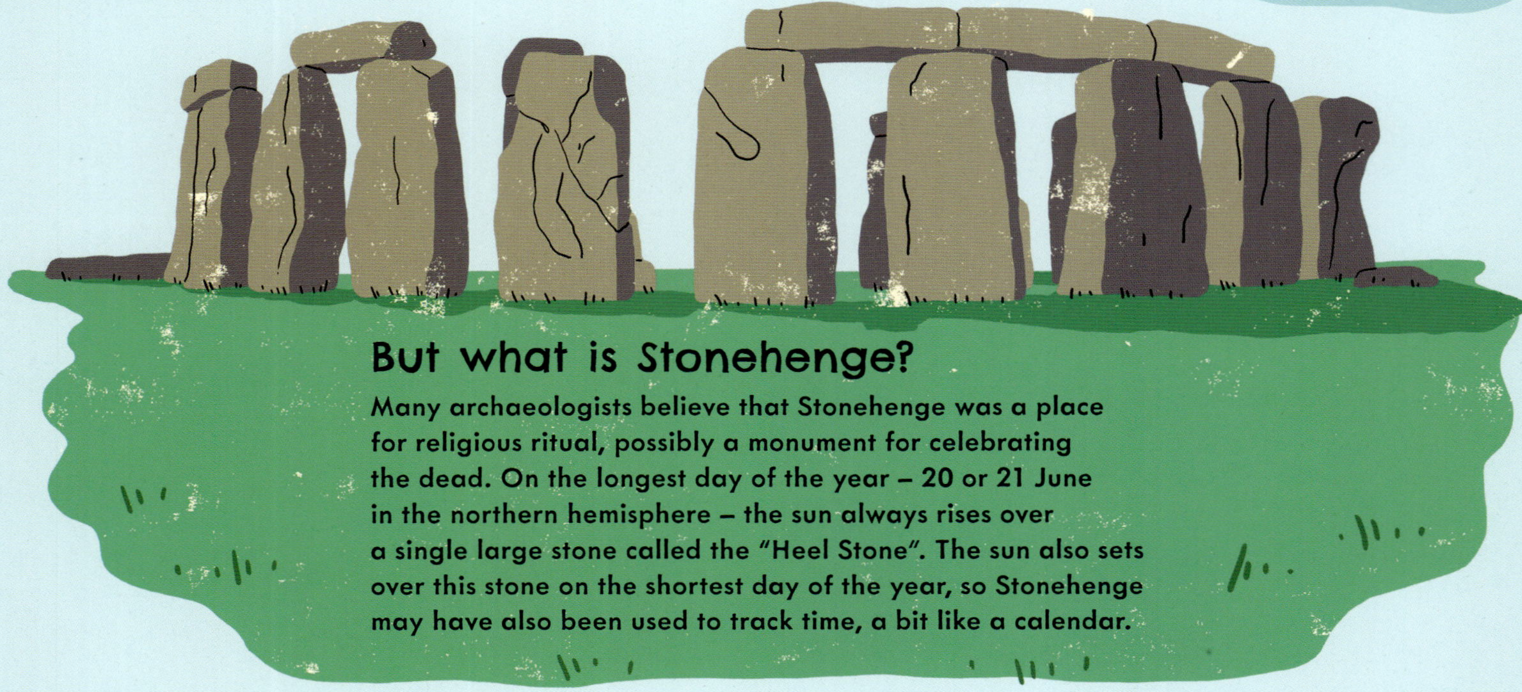

But what is Stonehenge?

Many archaeologists believe that Stonehenge was a place for religious ritual, possibly a monument for celebrating the dead. On the longest day of the year – 20 or 21 June in the northern hemisphere – the sun always rises over a single large stone called the "Heel Stone". The sun also sets over this stone on the shortest day of the year, so Stonehenge may have also been used to track time, a bit like a calendar.

Skara Brae

Skara Brae in Orkney, Scotland, is one of the UK's most remote Stone Age settlements. People lived here roughly 5,000 years ago, making this archaeological site older than Stonehenge and the pyramids of Giza in Egypt.

Skara Brae was only discovered in 1850, when a storm moved some of the earth surrounding the village. The people who lived here had made their own furniture, jewellery and dice to play games.

The people of Skara Brae grew crops, such as wheat and barley, and farmed animals, including cattle, sheep and pigs.

Most of the stone furniture has been preserved. Some of the rooms contain stone beds, shelves and the remains of fireplaces.

Ness of Brodgar

In 2003, archaeologists discovered a large notched stone in a place called the Ness of Brodgar in Orkney, Scotland. When they dug deeper, they started to uncover buildings – they had found a 5,000-year-old Neolithic village!

Humans first lived on Orkney about 10,000 years ago, but the landscape then was very different from how it is now. The sea level was roughly 45 metres lower than it is today, and many of the Scottish islands – including Orkney and some of the Inner Hebridean islands – were connected to the mainland. This means that a lot of the archaeological evidence that might tell us more about these early inhabitants is unfortunately deep underwater!

Every year, thousands of people visit the Ness of Brodgar to watch the archaeologists digging away. So far, archaeologists have recovered over 1,000 kg of pottery from the digs at this site!

Mount Sandel

The oldest evidence of humans living in Northern Ireland was found at Mount Sandel, an ancient campsite dating back 9,000 years. This Stone Age site straddles the banks of the River Bann.

The remains found at Mount Sandel suggest that people built tent-like structures using wood, reeds and animal hide. For food, they caught fish, including trout, salmon and eel, using spears and harpoons. They probably also hunted wild boar in the neighbouring woodland, and they may have collected hazelnuts to store so they could eat them in the colder months.

This ancient harpoon is made of wood and fragments of flint.

In June 2021, in Kilmartin Glen, Scotland, an archaeologist discovered carvings of deer that are believed to be 4,000 to 5,000 years old.

Barclodiad y Gawres

Around 150 early stone dwellings, called "cromlechi", still exist in Wales today, mostly along the west coast. Barclodiad y Gawres, meaning "the giantess's apronful", is one of the country's most impressive. Located on the island of Anglesey, it was used as a burial chamber. The tomb houses five stones decorated with spirals, zigzags and patterns, thought to be the earliest examples of art in Wales.

2,400 BCE – 43 CE

Tribes and communities

The Bronze Age

The Stone Age in Britain ended around 2,400 BCE, when the people living there learned how to extract metals from rocks to make bronze. This important discovery paved the way for the Bronze Age, which lasted until 800 BCE.

Beaker pottery

Beaker pottery first appeared in a region called Iberia (modern-day Spain and Portugal). While it is difficult to be sure, research suggests that the Beaker people came to Central Europe from the Eurasian Steppe, an area extending east from Central Europe across much of Central Asia. They are thought to have arrived in south-west England around 4,400 years ago, bringing their culture with them.

Bronze and gold

The use of bronze transformed architecture, weaponry and tool-making in the UK. In 1833, workers in Mold, a town in Flintshire, Wales, uncovered a spectacular gold cape thought to have been made in the early Bronze Age. You can see the Mold Gold Cape, one of the greatest pieces of metalworking from the prehistoric era, at the British Museum in London.

The Iron Age

By 800 BCE, people started to use iron to make tools and weapons, ushering in the Iron Age. The change made farming easier, and daily life in the UK transformed once again.

Tribes of Britain and Ireland

The Iron Age in Britain lasted for around 800 years. During this time, many people belonged to "tribes". A tribe is made up of groups of people who are often related to one another. They live in a specific area and share a common culture, language and leader.

We know that there were over 27 major tribes living throughout England, Scotland and Wales at this time. These collections of tribes are often referred to as "Celts". At the same time, numerous Celtic tribes were also settling on the island of Ireland.

In the Iron Age, people lived inside hill forts, in round houses made from "wattle" (sticks) and "daub" (a mixture of straw, clay and dung).

Most of the information historians have about these tribes comes from travelling Roman and Greek writers who came into contact with them. Historians also use coins as evidence. By studying coins used across the UK, historians have been able to roughly map where many of these tribes would have lived.

Historians gather evidence from as many different places as possible to try to understand the past. They ask important questions to figure out how trustworthy their source is.

Does it have a date?

Where was the evidence found?

If it's a written source, who wrote it and why?

Here are some tribes that were found across the UK at the close of the Iron Age . . .

The Picts

The Picts lived in what is now eastern and north-eastern Scotland. The word "Pict" comes from the Roman name *Picti*, meaning "painted people". The Picts are thought to have painted or tattooed their bodies. Many towns in Scotland still have Pictish names, such as Pittenweem and Pitlochry.

The Votadini lived in what is now south-east Scotland and north-east England. Their territory was conquered by the Roman army around 80 CE.

The Caledones lived in a region called Caledonia (modern-day Scotland).

The Ulaid lived in what is now north-eastern Ireland in the second century BCE.

The Demetae lived on small farms found across what is now south-west Wales.

Migration to the UK

When a person or group of people move from one place to settle in another, it is called "migration". The people who move are called "migrants".

Scientists studying ancient remains have discovered that, around 1,000 BCE, a huge number of people travelled from what is now known as France to England and Wales. This mass migration might help to explain why some French practices were adopted in Britain during this time.

The Trinovantes

When the Romans invaded Britain, one of the most powerful tribes were the Trinovantes, who lived in the area now known as Essex, England. The Trinovantes introduced some daily-life customs, such as eating from plates and drinking from cups.

The Romans invade Britain

Following its founding in 27 BCE, the Roman Empire expanded quickly, soon occupying huge stretches of land across Europe. The Romans were desperate to conquer Britain and take control of the valuable resources.

Invasions of Britain

The Roman leader Julius Caesar tried and failed to gain control of Britain twice. But, in 43 CE, the Romans invaded once more, this time led by Emperor Claudius. The powerful Roman army landed in Kent and marched to Colchester, where they claimed the territories of the Catuvellauni tribe, who ruled south-east England.

Not everyone welcomed Roman rule in Britain. Boudicca, the queen of the Iceni tribe in eastern England, led a revolt against the Romans in 60 CE. Although the rebellion was eventually quashed, it posed a massive threat to Roman forces. Even Londinium – the city we know today as London – fell to the Iceni at first.

It is thought that Boudicca's soldiers painted themselves blue for protection by their gods – it also made them look more threatening to their enemies!

The Roman army reached the Welsh borders around 48 CE. There, a man called Caractacus, or Caradoc in Welsh legend, led the resistance against the Romans. Although he and his troops put up a strong fight, they were eventually defeated at the Battle of Caer Caradoc in 50 CE.

Caractacus was captured and sent to Rome, but Emperor Claudius was so impressed by his courage that he pardoned him.

Ireland was known to the Romans as "Hibernia". The Romans never managed to invade Ireland, despite planning to in 81 CE. The Roman general Agricola was preparing his army in western Scotland, when another uprising forced him to abandon the invasion. Ireland still traded with Roman Britain, exchanging things such as metals, cattle and grains.

The tribes in Caledonia (Scotland) resisted Roman invasion, too, and some territories remained unconquered for several years. The Romans built two walls in an attempt to keep peace in the north. Hadrian's Wall was built on the orders of Emperor Hadrian after his visit in 122 CE. The ruins of the wall, which was an incredible 73 miles long, can still be seen today.

Diversity in Britain

The skeleton of a Roman woman, later known as the "Ivory Bangle Lady", was found in York in 1901, along with jewellery, a glass jug and a mirror. Research shows that the lady was likely a wealthy woman of North African descent who lived during the fourth century. This means that people from across the Roman Empire must have been living at this time in the area we now call England.

Further north, an inscription found near a fort at Burgh-by-Sands on Hadrian's Wall describes an African soldier who had been stationed there. These two discoveries tell us that a diverse community of people lived across Roman Britain.

The end of Roman Britain

After ruling Britain for over 400 years, the Romans eventually withdrew from the land in 410 CE, returning to Rome to defend their empire from powerful Germanic tribes called the "Visigoths".

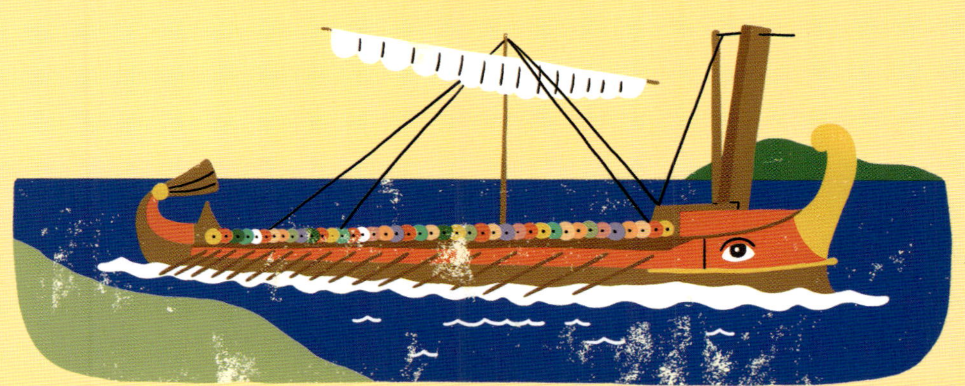

The Romans left a lasting impact on Britain. In fact, even the word "Britain" comes from the name the Romans used to describe the island – Britannia. Today, we can still see Roman influence on the UK and beyond.

Roman numerals are letters that the Romans used to represent numbers. We can often see these used on watches and clocks, or used in the names of our monarchs.

Latin was the language of ancient Rome and its empire. Many of our words and phrases come from Latin, like "villa", which means "house".

You can visit a well-preserved Roman bath, or "thermae", in the city of Bath, Somerset, England. The Romans didn't only use baths to get clean, but also as places to conduct business, socialize and relax.

The Romans were famous for building roads that were flat and straight. The Fosse Way is one of the longest and straightest Roman roads still in use in the UK today, running from the city of Exeter in southern England to Lincoln in the north-east.

Fantastic festivals

The people of the UK love a good party, whatever the season! Many of the celebrations enjoyed today have their roots in times gone by.

Hogmanay

The year starts with two Scottish festivals. Hogmanay, a raucous celebration of good cheer with toe-tapping ceilidhs and spectacular fireworks, is celebrated on New Year's Eve. To bring good luck, tradition says that the first person to visit any home after midnight should be a dark-haired man carrying coal, shortbread and whisky.

Burns Night

Just a few weeks later, on 25 January, many Scots come together to celebrate Burns Night. They share a supper in honour of national poet, Robert Burns, with haggis as the centrepiece.

St David's Day

Spring in the UK brings three important saints' days. The first is celebrated across Wales on 1 March to commemorate St David, known as Dewi Sant in Welsh. People dress up in traditional clothes and often wear a daffodil or a leek, both national symbols of Wales.

St Patrick's Day

On 17 March, there are widespread celebrations throughout Ireland and Northern Ireland, and many other countries worldwide in honour of St Patrick, patron saint of Ireland, who is buried at Downpatrick in County Down. On the day, many people wear green as parades fill the streets and traditional music is played.

St George's Day

On 23 April, it's the turn of the English with St George's Day. The most famous legend about St George claims he once slayed a dragon. Sometimes town-crier contests and puppet shows take place during the festivities.

May Day

On 1 May, a celebration going back over 2,000 years is held across the UK. The ancient roots of May Day can be traced to the time of the Celts, who welcomed it as the first day of summer. To celebrate, a May Queen is crowned and Morris dancers perform. 1 May is also International Worker's Day, where people honour workers around the world and campaign for fair working conditions and pay.

Notting Hill Carnival

A celebration of Caribbean culture and heritage, the Notting Hill Carnival has taken place in London, at the end of August since 1966. There are colourful costumes, an array of music and over 200 food stalls selling everything from curried goat to jerk chicken.

Guy Fawkes Night

In 1605, a man named Guy Fawkes hatched the Gunpowder Plot – a plan to blow up the Houses of Parliament in London with King James I inside. On 5 November, his plan failed, and Guy Fawkes and his followers were all caught and executed.

In Britain today, Guy Fawkes Night is often called Bonfire Night and is more about watching fantastic fireworks than celebrating a failed assassination. But from 1606 until 1859, British people were required by law to commemorate this event! Some people still throw a scarecrow, or "Guy", on to their fires to represent Guy Fawkes.

Pride

The first official UK Gay Pride rally was held in London in 1972, when a crowd of 2,000 came together to celebrate their identities and stand up against violence and intimidation towards gay people. Pride marches today are held by LGBTQ+ people and allies across the UK throughout the year, with London's parade – one of the largest in the country – generally taking place in the summer.

Diwali

Diwali is a light-filled autumn festival, which is celebrated by Hindus, Sikhs and Jains all over the UK and the world. In Leicester, England, the streets are strung with glittering lights and fireworks fill the sky.

St Andrew's Day

At the end of November, Scots celebrate St Andrew's Day. People gather together to listen to music and eat traditional food, such as a fishy soup called Cullen skink. According to Christian religion, St Andrew was one of the twelve disciples of Jesus Christ. Despite becoming the patron saint of Scotland, he never actually visited the country during his lifetime.

The Anglo-Saxons

The Anglo-Saxons were migrants from northern Europe. They included tribes from northern Germany, southern Denmark and the Netherlands, with the three biggest groups being the Angles, the Saxons and the Jutes.

After the Romans left, small parties of warriors came to fight the Britons. They were followed by others who simply wanted to farm Britain's fertile land, as their own lands were prone to flooding.

The word "England" comes from the Saxon word meaning "land of the Angles".

Kings and kingdoms

Mercia was one of seven Anglo-Saxon kingdoms. In the year 825, Egbert (Ecgberht) defeated the king of Mercia, Beornwulf, and soon controlled much of southern England and eventually even northern Wales. It wasn't until a century later in 927, during the reign of King Athelstan, the first king of England, that the Anglo-Saxons were joined in a single region, England.

Bernicia was the most northern Anglo-Saxon kingdom in what we would recognize as southern Scotland today.

Beowulf is an epic poem from this period and one of the first-ever pieces of Old English literature. It tells the story of a brave hero who kills a dragon and the poem has over 3,000 lines!

The Battle of Hastings

When the Vikings arrived in 793, they posed a big threat to the Anglo-Saxons, who faced constant attacks.

In October 1066, William of Normandy arrived on British shores to challenge Harold II for the throne. During the infamous Battle of Hastings, William's Norman army defeated and killed Harold II, marking the end of Anglo-Saxon rule in Britain.

Harold II was the last Anglo-Saxon king of England.

The Vikings

793

1066

The departure of the Romans left Britain unstable and vulnerable to invasions. Tribes from other parts of Europe seized the opportunity to attack and settle in the region. One such tribe came from the region we know today as Scandinavia, made up of Norway, Sweden and Denmark: the Vikings.

Historians disagree about where the name "Viking" comes from. It means "pirate raid" in Old Norse, the language the Vikings spoke. Many English words have their roots in Old Norse, such as "glitter" and "cake".

The first Viking raid on Britain was recorded in 793. In the years that followed, these Scandinavian pirates continued to raid the coasts of England, Scotland, Wales and Northern Ireland, attacking large monasteries with precious treasures, such as silver and gold.

Not only were the Vikings fierce fighters, but they were also skilled at crafting, trading and building boats. One of the most impressive Viking ships was the "longship", known for its great speed and ability to sail in choppy waters.

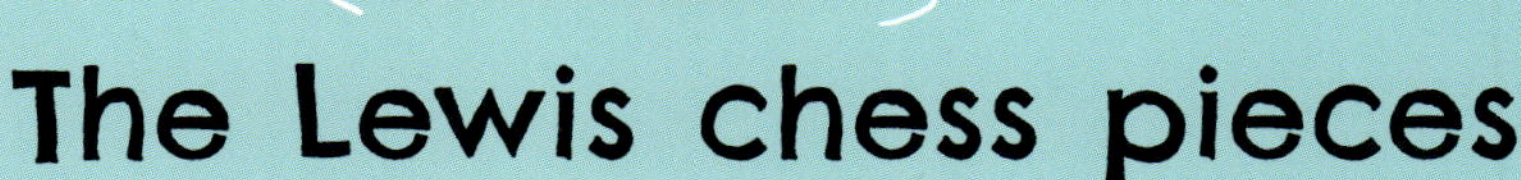

The Lewis chess pieces

In 1831, the Lewis chess pieces were found on a beach in Uig on the Isle of Lewis, in Scotland. Carved from the teeth of sperm whales and walrus ivory, these impressive objects were probably made in Norway in the late twelfth or early thirteenth century.

It's likely they were buried by a merchant planning to trade them. Their discovery shows that the ties between Scandinavia and Scotland remained strong beyond the Viking era.

The Vikings believed in many gods, including Loki, a trickster who could shapeshift, and Thor, the god of thunder. Some of the English names for days of the week come from the names of Norse gods. For example, Thursday is named after Thor.

The Vikings (continued)

Settlement

By the end of the ninth century, the Vikings had begun to settle across Britain, mainly in north and eastern parts of England. In 866, they took over York and declared it their capital, renaming the city "Jorvik".

Alfred, King of Wessex, battled the Vikings several times, and in 878 his army won. He later signed a treaty with Guthrum, the Danish king who led the invasion against him. The treaty formally divided England between the Vikings and the English. The Viking land became known as the "Danelaw".

The Vikings left behind plenty of evidence in the Northern Isles of Scotland! Over 30 runic inscriptions, a type of Viking graffiti, were found at Maeshowe in Orkney. It is one of the largest known collections of runes in Europe.

In the ninth century, Viking encampments were scattered throughout the island of Ireland. The Vikings founded important cities in Ireland, including Dublin. In 1014, Brian Boru, High King of Ireland, defeated a Viking army at Clontarf.

The Vikings also settled in south-west Wales. They never took control of the region, but many places in Wales have Norse origins, like the island of Worms Head on the Gower Peninsula. The Vikings gave the island this name because they thought it was a sleeping dragon – "worm" means "dragon" in Old Norse!

Viking raids on what is now the UK continued for hundreds of years. Sweyn Forkbeard, king of Denmark, invaded England in 1013 and became its ruler. However, he was only king for five short weeks before he suddenly died. His son Canute (Cnut the Great) took over. During Canute's reign, England officially became part of the Scandinavian kingdom.

End of the Viking age

The final Viking invasion took place in 1066, when Harald Hardrada, the king of Norway, marched to Stamford Bridge near York in an attempt to win the English throne after the death of King Edward the Confessor. The new English king, Harold II, defeated Hardrada after a gruelling battle. With this victory, the age of the Vikings in Britain came to an end.

1066–1154

The Normans

The Normans were Vikings who had settled in northern France. After William of Normandy was victorious in the Battle of Hastings, first England, then Wales, Scotland and parts of Ireland, fell under Norman control and influence. The region began to experience big changes in lifestyle, culture, architecture and economics.

Historians can often tell where Normans lived because of their unique motte-and-bailey castles. These castles were made from timber, and many are still standing today. Unlike stone castles, motte-and-bailey castles were cheap and fast to build.

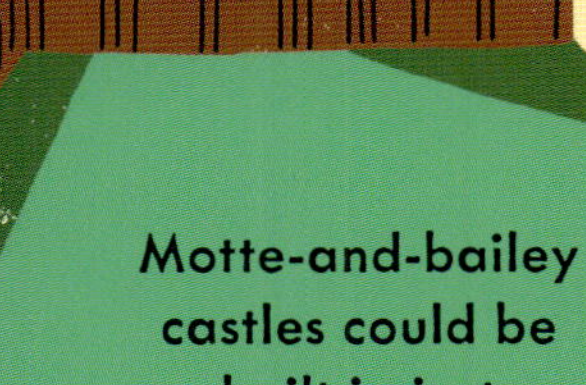

In 1085, William of Normandy ordered a large-scale survey to gather information about who held land throughout England and parts of Wales. The *Domesday Book* is a treasure trove of information for historians. It is very detailed, giving an incredibly clear snapshot of eleventh-century English society.

Table manners were very important to the Normans. If you needed to burp, you had to look up at the ceiling to avoid being impolite!

The Norman occupation led to many French words entering the English vocabulary. In fact, around a third of all English words we use today come from French, including "encore" and "chef".

William of Normandy brought the feudal system to England, which ranked people by their power within society. Under feudalism, the king, William, was the most powerful and owned all the land in the region. Those below him were granted land but only in return for their money, protection or service.

The Bayeux Tapestry

The Bayeux Tapestry is a piece of embroidered cloth that shows the epic story of the Norman victory at the Battle of Hastings in 1066. It is almost 70 metres long and 50 centimetres tall and is on display in Bayeux, France. However, in 1885 a group of skilled Victorian women created a copy of the tapestry so the UK could have a version, too.

Kings and queens

Today, the whole UK is ruled by one king or queen, but this wasn't always the case. Long ago, the lands were divided between many rival groups, each with their own leader. Towards the end of the ninth century, Alfred, King of Wessex, also known as Alfred the Great, united much of England under his rule. Here are just a few famous kings and queens.

Royal families

William of Normandy ruled over England from 1066 until his death in 1087. After William's reign, the crown was handed down through families, creating dynasties. Six main dynasties have held the English throne, and later English monarchs ruled over Wales, Scotland and Northern Ireland, too. How many of these kings and queens have you heard of?

Alfred the Great
Lived: 849–899
Reigned: 871–899

William I
Dynasty: Norman
Lived: 1028–1087
Reigned: 1066–1087

Richard I
Dynasty: Plantagenet
Lived: 1157–1199
Reigned: 1189–1199

Richard I reigned for ten years, but he only spent around seven months in the UK! He was often away at war or on crusades.

Henry V
Dynasty: Plantagenet
Lived: 1387–1422
Reigned: 1413–1422

Richard III
Dynasty: Plantagenet
Lived: 1452–1485
Reigned: 1483–1485

In 1536, Henry VIII introduced a law that united England and Wales – but he's much more famous for having six wives, two of whom he had beheaded (see page 31).

Henry VIII
Dynasty: Tudor
Lived: 1491–1547
Reigned: 1509–1547

Mary I
Dynasty: Tudor
Lived: 1516–1558
Reigned: 1553–1558

Elizabeth I
Dynasty: Tudor
Lived: 1533–1603
Reigned: 1558–1603

James became the king of England in 1603, but he had already been the king of Scotland since 1567, where he was known as James VI.

James I
Dynasty: Stuart
Lived: 1566–1625
Reigned: 1603–1625

Charles I is the only British king ever to have been executed, and his reign ended in civil war. After Charles I's death, Oliver Cromwell became Lord Protector, and England didn't have a monarch for eleven years.

Charles I
Dynasty: Stuart
Lived: 1600–1649
Reigned: 1625–1649

William III and Mary II
Dynasty: Stuart
William lived: 1650–1702
Mary lived: 1662–1694
Reigned: 1689–1702

Victoria
Dynasty: Hanover
Lived: 1819–1901
Reigned: 1837–1901

Queen Victoria was the leader of the largest empire in history, claiming to rule over more than 450 million people. During Victoria's reign, the British Empire reached as far as Australia, New Zealand, Canada, South Africa and India.

Queen Elizabeth II was the longest-reigning British monarch ever, celebrating 70 years on the throne in 2022. On Elizabeth II's death, her son Charles was pronounced king, becoming King Charles III.

Elizabeth II
Dynasty: Windsor
Lived: 1926–2022
Reigned: 1952–2022

Medieval war

The Normans fought hard to assert their power and widen their reach across British and Irish society. But wars and rebellions raged on throughout the medieval period, causing massive upheaval.

The invasion of Armagh

In 1176, a Norman army invaded Armagh in what is now Northern Ireland, but the Irish fought back, killing over 500 Norman soldiers.

Dozens of battles took place between England and Scotland during the medieval era, and the borders of the regions changed constantly.

Llywelyn the Last

Llywelyn the Last was the prince of a region called Gwynedd in northern Wales. Desperate to maintain Welsh independence, he fought hard to keep the English out. But, soon after his death in 1282, all of Wales fell under English rule.

The Declaration of Arbroath

The Declaration of Arbroath is a famous letter written in 1320 by Scottish barons. Writing of the need for an independent Scotland, the barons asked the Pope for help to end the Wars of Scottish Independence. After many years, the wars eventually ended in 1357 with the signing of the Treaty of Berwick.

Christianity and the Crusades

Christianity became a huge part of daily life in the medieval period, and the Church had a lot of influence. Christian children were baptized, and people attended mass services every Sunday.

Religion played a key part in the politics of Europe, too. In 1096, the first in a series of religious wars called the "Crusades" was fought in Eastern Europe and the Middle East. Christians and Muslims battled for control of sacred sites such as Jerusalem. There were at least eight Crusades in total and, in 1291, the wars eventually ended with Muslim victory in the Middle East.

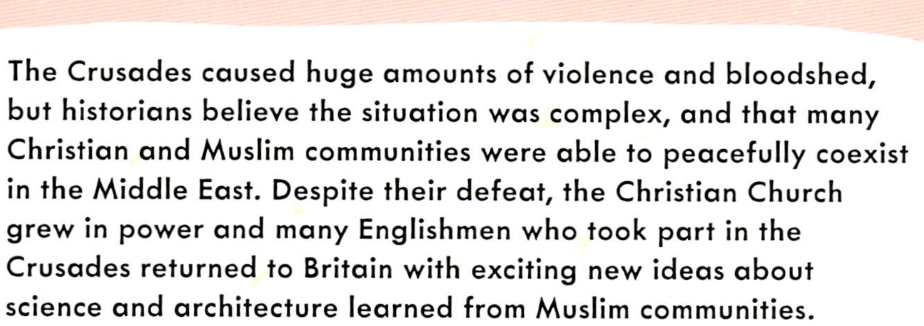

The Crusades caused huge amounts of violence and bloodshed, but historians believe the situation was complex, and that many Christian and Muslim communities were able to peacefully coexist in the Middle East. Despite their defeat, the Christian Church grew in power and many Englishmen who took part in the Crusades returned to Britain with exciting new ideas about science and architecture learned from Muslim communities.

The Black Death in Britain

Between 1347 and 1351, a deadly pandemic called the Black Death swept through Europe. Most scientists believe the disease was carried by infected rats, and that it was passed on to humans through flea bites. The unpleasant symptoms ranged from a sudden fever and chills to painful, swollen lymph nodes called "buboes".

The Black Death had a devastating impact. It is thought to have killed around 30 to 45 per cent of the population between 1348 and 1350. Entire villages fell victim to the plague, although there were slightly fewer deaths in Scotland and Northern Ireland compared to England and Wales.

A pandemic is an infectious disease that spreads widely, often affecting the whole world over many months.

Plague doctors wore masks that looked like beaks. Doctors put herbs and dried flowers such as mint and roses in the mask to try and keep away bad smells.

The Peasants' Revolt

The staggering death toll from the Black Death not only led to a shortage of workers, but it also saw peasants grow desperate for better rights and higher wages.

With the economy in tatters and wars to finance, the government placed several taxes on the rich and poor between 1377 and 1381. The poll tax of 1381 was the final straw, sparking the Peasants' Revolt in England in June that year. A group of peasants marched to the Tower of London to demand reforms from the king.

While the revolt failed, it remains an important event in English history and is believed to be the first people's rebellion in the UK.

A clash of crowns

Ongoing wars with France, and struggles for the crown at home made way for a bitter civil war in England, resulting in the rise of a powerful family – the House of Tudor.

The Hundred Years' War

A civil war occurs when citizens of the same country take sides and fight each other.

The English had been fighting with the French on and off ever since the Norman Conquest of 1066. The peak of this feud was known as the Hundred Years' War, confusingly lasting 116 years. The tension reached breaking point at the Battle of Agincourt in 1415.

A longbow was a single curved bow up to 2 metres long that shot arrows twice as far as a short bow and inflicted more damage.

The heavy armour worn by the French soldiers made them sink in the boggy mud that covered the battlefield.

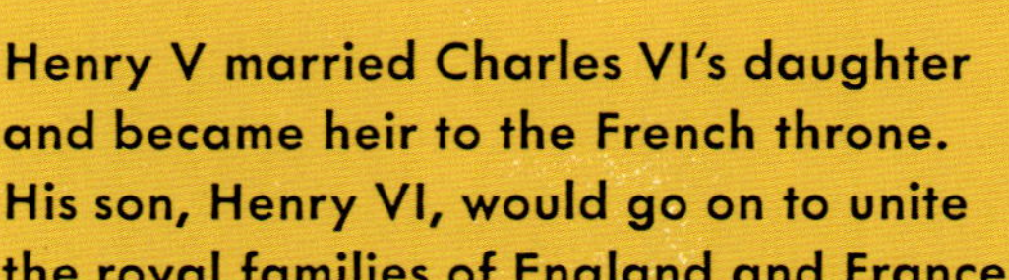

The English won the battle. Instead of taking prisoners, King Henry V ordered his men to kill all of the French knights, even those who had surrendered.

Henry V married Charles VI's daughter and became heir to the French throne. His son, Henry VI, would go on to unite the royal families of England and France.

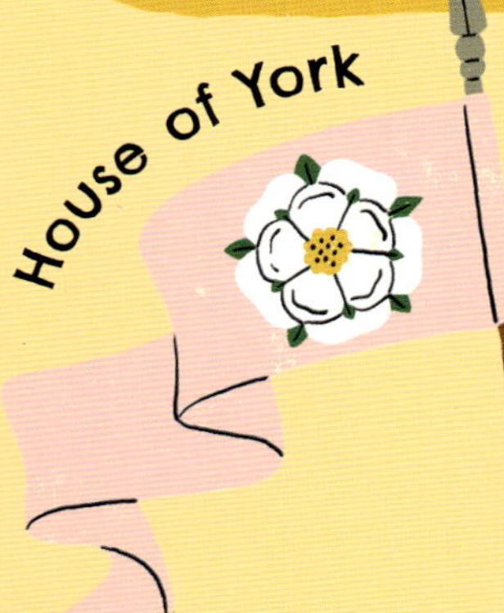

The Wars of the Roses

Two royal houses, the House of York and the House of Lancaster, fought one another for the right to rule from 1455 to 1485 – the longest period of civil war in English history. It was an epic family feud, as the people in both houses were descended from the sons of one man, King Edward III.

The Battle of Bosworth, near Leicester, ended the wars. Henry Tudor fought Richard III for the English throne. During the battle, Richard got knocked off his horse and killed in a bog, making him the last English king to die on the battlefield.

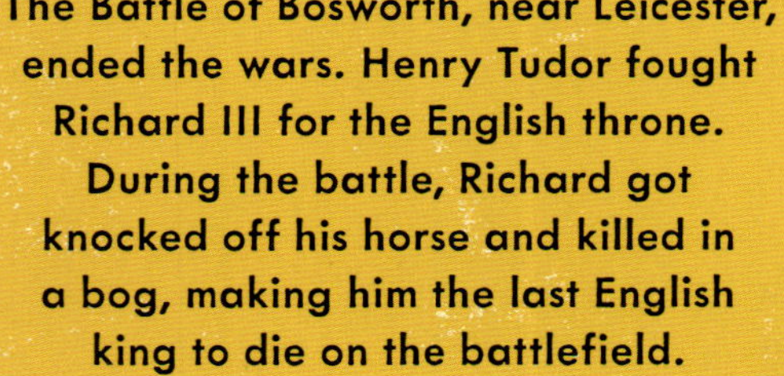

In 2012 archaeologists were amazed to discover Richard's skeleton underneath a car park in Leicestershire, England!

The victorious King Henry Tudor married Elizabeth of York in 1486, finally uniting the York and Lancaster families and beginning the powerful Tudor dynasty.

Henry VIII

Henry was exceptionally tall for the time and wore the finest robes and suits of armour.

Henry VIII was born in 1491 and became king aged just eighteen. He excelled at music, languages, poetry and sports.

Power was held by men at this time, and Henry needed a male heir to secure the Tudor dynasty. He and his first wife Catherine of Aragon had several baby boys who died. With no son in sight, Catherine was banished.

Henry's next marriage to Anne Boleyn in 1533 outraged members of the Catholic church, who were shocked at his divorce from Catherine. Divorce didn't really exist at this time and was relatively unheard of until Henry came along!

The Catholic church disagreed with Henry's new marriage, so to solve this, he made himself leader of a new Protestant church and seized wealth from hundreds of Catholic monasteries (buildings in which monks live). When Anne failed to provide a son, he accused her of witchcraft and had her beheaded at the Tower of London.

In 1536, Henry fell from a horse and was badly injured. Following the accident, he became angry and violent, imprisoning and executing those seen as a threat.

During his reign, Henry VIII made many changes, including establishing the Royal Navy, which had over 40 battleships by the time he died in 1547.

Henry VIII had six wives in all. This rhyme can be used to remember what happened to them:

DIVORCED	BEHEADED	DIED	DIVORCED	BEHEADED	SURVIVED
Catherine of Aragon	Anne Boleyn	Jane Seymour	Anne of Cleves	Kathryn Howard	Catherine Parr

Explosive power

1558

1605

Henry VIII's heirs, Edward VI and Mary I, each died after only a short time on the throne. England's next monarch was another of Henry VIII's children, Elizabeth I. But she had to struggle against her cousin Mary, Queen of Scots, for the crown. The Scottish Reformation and the foiling of the Gunpowder Plot confirmed Scotland and England as Protestant.

Elizabeth vs Mary

Elizabeth I and Mary, Queen of Scots, were cousins. They had a fierce rivalry.

Elizabeth I was known as the "Virgin Queen" as she vowed never to marry.

I was born in 1533. My father, Henry VIII, had my mother, Anne Boleyn, beheaded. I was shunned and ignored as a child. However, my outstanding intelligence helped me stand out from the crowd.

During Elizabeth's long reign as queen of England (1558–1603), theatre and the arts flourished and William Shakespeare became popular.

Elizabeth died in 1603. Some believe that the iconic white make-up that she used steadily poisoned her.

I was born in 1542 and became queen of Scotland at just six days old. The kings of England and France each plotted to marry me in order to control Scotland. When I was six, I was sent to France and promised to their dauphin (future king). I was pampered with pretty dresses, dancing, riding and singing lessons.

Murder, captivity & death

Mary returned to Scotland in 1561. Her second husband mysteriously died in a fire, and, when she married the Earl of Bothwell shortly after, they were both suspected of murder.

Her enemies ran her out of Scotland in 1568. Mary expected her cousin to offer help. Instead, Elizabeth had her imprisoned for nineteen years. When Mary attempted to smuggle an escape letter in a beer barrel, a spy network discovered that she was plotting to kill Elizabeth.

Mary was beheaded at Fotheringhay Castle in 1587. The executioner held up her head for the crowd to see. It fell to the floor, leaving him holding just her wig!

The first colonists

Seafarers Walter Raleigh and Francis Drake were some of Elizabeth's favourite courtiers. She supported their attempts to set up colonies in the Americas.

Raleigh went in search of "El Dorado", the mythical city of gold in South America. His plan was scuppered, however, when he broke a peace treaty with France in 1617. He was executed a year later.

Drake became a sailor when he was twelve and joined one of England's first fleets, trafficking people from Africa to be enslaved in the Americas. He played a part in defeating the Spanish Armada in 1588 and saving England from invasion. The Spanish were angry at Drake for raiding and burning their ships. Despite the Spanish Armada having a much stronger and larger fleet, around 130 ships and 19,000 soldiers, the English army had more guns and boats better suited to the stormy weather.

WANTED

The Scottish Reformation

Many people disliked the Catholic Church. They believed it was misusing its power and wanted changes to be made. John Knox was born around 1514 in Scotland. His fiery speeches encouraged people to destroy Catholic churches.

In the *Book of Discipline*, several authors, including Knox, called for greater equality and care for the poor. In 1560, the Church of Scotland officially became Protestant.

The Nine Years' War

Between 1593 and 1603, the English fought against Gaelic Irish clan leaders. The English were victorious, they seized Irish land and tried to make Ireland a Protestant country. This marked the end of Gaelic Ireland.

The Gunpowder Plot of 1605

After Elizabeth I died, James VI of Scotland united the English and Scottish crowns and became James I of England. As a Protestant, he clamped down harshly on Catholics in England. A group of Catholic men, led by Robert Catesby, plotted to blow up the Houses of Parliament and kill not just the king, but everyone in the government. Their secret was discovered before they could act, and they were arrested and executed (see page 21).

There were 36 barrels of gunpowder discovered beneath Parliament – enough to kill hundreds of people!

Every year on 5 November, people all over the UK mark the failure of the plot with bonfires and firework displays.

A land of literature

Books, plays and poems can transport us to different places and times. Take a literary journey through the ages with some of the UK's most beloved writers.

Geoffrey Chaucer
1342–1400

Most authors of Chaucer's time wrote in French or Latin, but Chaucer chose to write in English so that more people could understand his work. His most famous work, *The Canterbury Tales*, is a collection of stories about a group of pilgrims, including a knight, a cook and a monk. Some tales are funny and rude, whereas others are serious and sad!

William Shakespeare
1564–1616

The son of a glove maker, William Shakespeare was born in Stratford-upon-Avon, England. In his lifetime, Shakespeare wrote at least 38 plays and over 150 poems. They became famous all over the world, and we still use many interesting phrases from them today, including . . .

The world is my oyster.

break the ice

Love is blind.

wild goose chase

own flesh and blood

Olaudah Equiano
1745–1797

Equiano was kidnapped, enslaved and brought to England from Essaka (Nigeria) as a child. He was eventually able to buy his freedom, and he wrote about his experiences. His influential autobiography, *The Interesting Narrative of the Life of Olaudah Equiano*, helped to end slavery.

Robert Burns
1759–1796

The national poet of Scotland Robert Burns wrote poems and songs in Scots language. One of his most famous poems, "Address to a Haggis", was written in appreciation of the savoury pudding traditionally made from an animal's stomach stuffed with offal, oats and spices.

Beatrix Potter
1866–1943

The creator of Peter Rabbit, Beatrix Potter lived in the Lake District, England, with a whole menagerie of animals, including rabbits, hedgehogs, frogs, mice and bats. Her pets and the landscapes near her home inspired her well-loved children's books.

Agatha Christie
1890–1976

The queen of crime stories, Agatha Christie created not one but two famous detectives in her work – Hercule Poirot and Miss Marple. Her play *The Mousetrap* is the longest-running theatre production in history! It has been watched by ten million theatregoers since it opened in 1952.

C. S. Lewis
1898–1963

Creator of the magical world of Narnia, C. S. Lewis was born in Belfast, Northern Ireland. He was a big fan of Beatrix Potter's stories, which inspired the talking animals in his own work.

Benjamin Zephaniah
1958–2023

Writer and performance poet Benjamin Zephaniah grew up between England and Jamaica. He wrote for children and adults, and his "dub poetry" – poetry set to a beat – explores important issues including racism and animal cruelty.

Here are some more names of famous UK writers. Have you read any of their books?

The early empire

By the late sixteenth century, England began to expand its influence over the word, and the first permanent colonies were established in North America. Meanwhile, wealth from the East India Company brought great profits from trade in Asia.

The "Lost Colony" of Roanoke

Roanoke, in what is now North Carolina in the United States, was England's first colony in North America. Sir Richard Grenville led an expedition of seven ships in 1585 to set up a military base and claim the land. The men were welcomed and fed by the Roanoke people.

When a silver cup disappeared, Grenville blamed the Indigenous Aquascogoc people. He torched their village and destroyed their community.

By 1590, the colonists had disappeared completely and people are still trying to solve this curious mystery.

Jamestown, Virginia

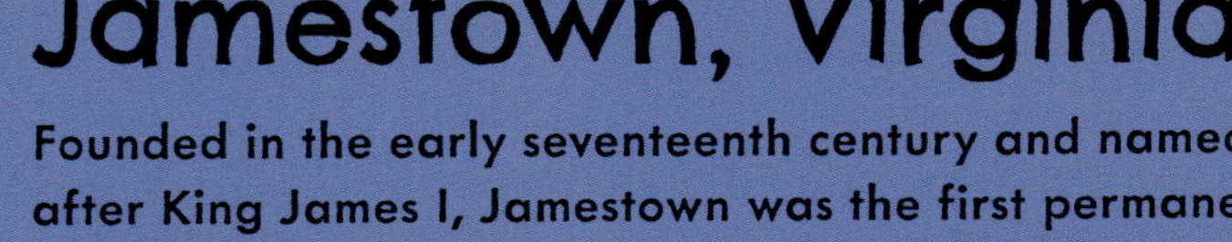

Founded in the early seventeenth century and named after King James I, Jamestown was the first permanent English colony in the Americas. The area was already inhabited by the Powhatan Confederacy, whose ancestors had lived there for thousands of years, and whose traditions continue today, with eleven recognized tribes living in modern-day Virginia.

When Captain John Smith arrived with a group of sailors in 1607, the Powhatan people were concerned. There was little food to go round and the English pressured the Powhatans to provide them with whatever food supplies they had. This conflict led to the first Anglo-Powhatan War.

New diseases, such as smallpox and influenza (the flu), killed many Indigenous peoples.

Pocahontas, Virginia

Amonute (nicknamed "Pocahontas") was the daughter of the chief of the Powhatan Confederacy. The colonists took her hostage in 1613, instructed her in English and baptized her "Rebecca" in 1616.

As part of the peace treaty, to end the first Anglo-Powhatan war, she was married to Englishman John Rolfe, the first person to cultivate tobacco for a profit. They came to England with their young son. Amonute died of smallpox in 1617.

The English took more and more Powhatan land to grow tobacco until, in 1622, Opechancanough, a chief of the Powhatan Confederacy, led an attack on their colony. In 1623, the English invited the leaders of the area to a "peace" conference, where they poisoned the wine and killed everyone.

The Mayflower

In 1620, a ship called the *Mayflower* arrived in a region that is now called New England, USA. The passengers were English pilgrims called "Puritans", who had been banished from England for their ways of worship. Arriving hungry in a place that was eventually renamed Plymouth, they stole the winter food rations of the Wampanoag people, whose ancestors had lived there for over 12,000 years.

The Wampanoag taught the colonists survival skills in return for weapons, but the English eventually stole their land. Only six out of the original 69 groups of Wampanoag people survived.

In 1619, the *White Lion* ship took at least 20 people from a Spanish slaving ship and brought them to Virginia. They were traded for food supplies and forced to work as servants.

The East India Company

The East India Company (EIC) was set up by English merchants and sailors in 1600 and authorized by Queen Elizabeth I to trade with Asia. The company wanted the expensive spices that the Dutch were taking from the islands in the East Indies, but they instead turned to the quick profits of fabrics and tea made in India.

The EIC enslaved people, provoked wars with China and eventually controlled around half of the world's trade. After the First War of Indian Independence (1857–1874), the British government closed the company, dissolving it entirely in 1874.

The EIC armies forced Indian people to work for low wages and to pay taxes. By 1800, the company had 200,000 soldiers.

The British men who came home from India with huge fortunes were called "nabobs".

Powis Castle in Wales has a huge collection of objects looted from India, including a bejewelled gold tiger head that belonged to ruler Tipu Sultan.

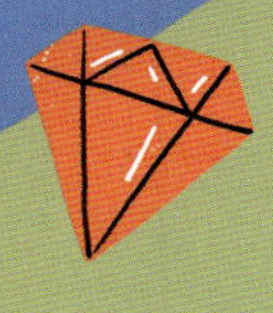

Civil war and unrest

The English Civil War, fought between the Roundheads and the Cavaliers, brought great disruption to the British Isles. Shortly after, most of London was burned down in a devastating fire. In this time of great change, women were unfairly accused of witchcraft.

King Charles I

Born in Dunfermline Palace in Scotland in 1600, King Charles I became king of England, Scotland and Ireland in 1625. Because his wife, Henrietta Maria of France, was Catholic, people worried that he favoured Catholicism. Charles believed that the "divine right of kings" allowed him to make decisions without consulting anyone else, including Parliament.

From 1629 to 1640, Charles ruled without calling Parliament once.

Charles made people pay taxes to fund an expensive war with Spain. If you didn't pay up, you were sent to jail!

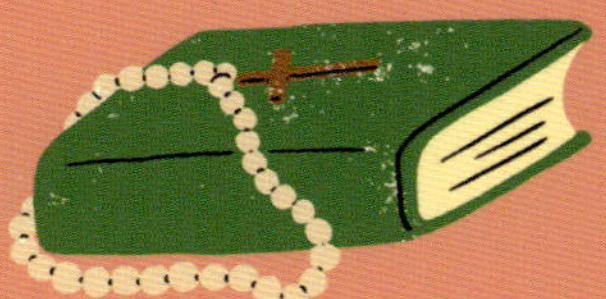

He angered Scottish people when he introduced the Book of Common Prayer in 1637, forcing them to worship the same way as the English and accept him as the head of the church. The Scots who refused, "Covenanters", were threatened with death.

Witchcraft and witch-hunts

In Europe, during this period of war, disease and great disruption, some people imagined that evil witches were to blame. Across the UK, more than 3,000 innocent people, mainly women, were accused of witchcraft and suffered grisly torture and death.

Professional witch prickers inserted needles into suspects' bodies and said they had a "witch's mark" if they found a spot that didn't bleed.

In 1662, John Dickson, a notorious, well-paid witch pricker in Scotland, was suspected of fraud and arrested. However, when John arrived at jail, he turned out to be a woman called Christian Caddell.

It is often thought that the last witch trial in the UK was in Dornoch, Scotland, in 1727. However, more than two centuries later, Helen Duncan was arrested in 1944 under the Witchcraft Act. The Witchcraft Acts were finally repealed in 1951.

The English Civil War

In England in the seventeenth century, the Cavaliers (who supported King Charles I) fought the Roundheads (who supported Parliament). The Roundheads were led by Oliver Cromwell.

Three big wars erupted between 1642 and 1651, known as the "Wars of the Three Kingdoms". Men from England, Scotland, Wales and Ireland were involved. A few women acted as spies or dressed as male soldiers.

The 22,000 soldiers who formed Cromwell's New Model Army in 1645 were chosen for their fighting skills and discipline.

In 1646, King Charles I expected to make a deal with the Scots and get their support, but in 1647 they captured him and handed him over to the Roundheads.

The years of fighting divided families and communities. Soldiers went on looting sprees and many castles were damaged or destroyed.

When Cromwell's army invaded Ireland in 1649, the consequences were devastating. Around 20 per cent of the population were killed, died from hunger or were exiled.

Betrayal and beheadings

In 1649, Charles I was beheaded for treason (the crime of betraying your own country). In 1653, Cromwell got rid of Parliament and appointed himself "Lord Protector", rather like a king. Cromwell died in 1658.

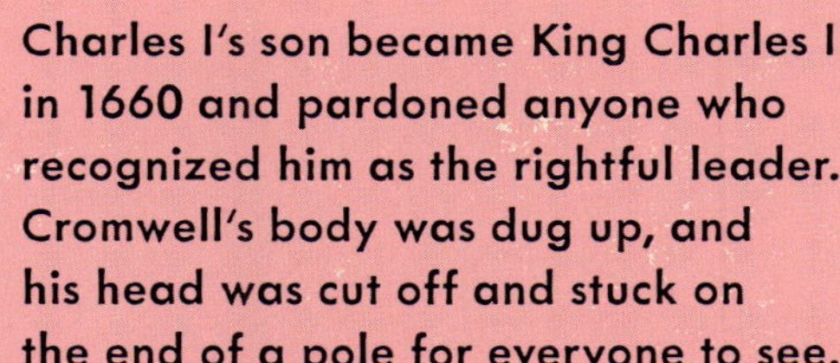

Charles I's son became King Charles II in 1660 and pardoned anyone who recognized him as the rightful leader. Cromwell's body was dug up, and his head was cut off and stuck on the end of a pole for everyone to see.

The Fire of London

In September 1666, a fire started in a baker's shop on Pudding Lane in London. There was no fire brigade at that time, so people used buckets of water to try to extinguish it. The fire raged across the city for four days, until the Navy blew up some buildings with gunpowder to stop the fire from spreading! Some 13,000 houses, 87 churches and many other very important buildings were destroyed. It took 30 years to rebuild the city.

Out of the ashes

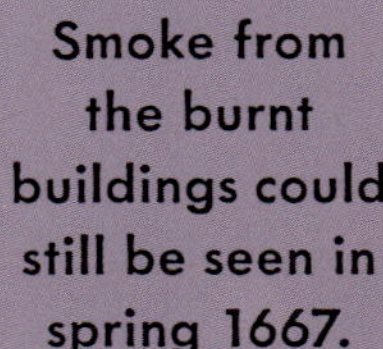

After recovering from the Fire of London, talented architects designed new buildings across the British Isles. Theatres reopened and writers and artists were given more creative freedom. This sparked a period of immense change in society, and ordinary people fought to improve their rights and freedoms.

1666

1730

London in ruins

After the Fire of London, 100,000 people were homeless. The cost of rent skyrocketed. Many people ended up in refugee camps, and a quarter of the population left London for good.

Collections at churches all over England and Wales raised money for those in need. On 10 October 1666, King Charles II ordered a special day of fasting. Heavy rain fell for ten days and helped to put out the embers strewn across the city.

Smoke from the burnt buildings could still be seen in spring 1667.

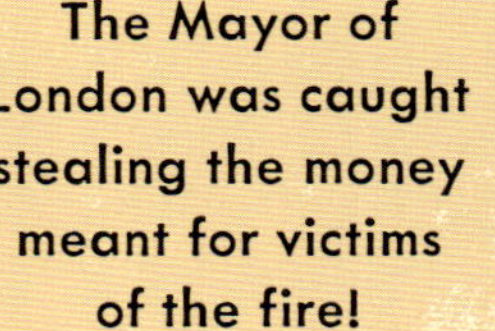

The Mayor of London was caught stealing the money meant for victims of the fire!

London is rebuilt

Christopher Wren was a brilliant scientist, mathematician and inventor. His new design for London contained wide avenues and more space between the houses to prevent fires from spreading.

King Charles II hired him as part of a team to help rebuild London. Wren's plans replaced wood with stone and removed the disgusting open sewers that carried human waste and spread disease.

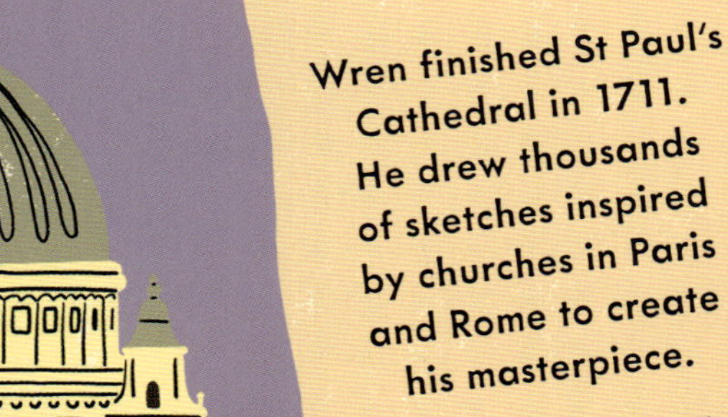

Wren finished St Paul's Cathedral in 1711. He drew thousands of sketches inspired by churches in Paris and Rome to create his masterpiece.

From Interregnum to Restoration

King Charles II came to power in 1660 and used art to show that the royal family was back in charge after the Interregnum (the time when no monarch ruled). He hired artists who glorified him in their extravagant paintings.

Artists and writers had more freedom to express their ideas. Theatres were allowed to open once more, and people enjoyed going to laugh at short comedies. Many famous books were written at this time, including *The Pilgrim's Progress* by John Bunyan, *Paradise Lost* by John Milton and compilations of poetry by John Dryden.

People wanted to have fun again. Sometimes, people gambled and won or lost money playing cards, chess, backgammon, dice and dominoes.

Art, especially paintings of landscapes and "still life" (objects), became particularly popular.

Crowds flocked to see free shows and unusual curiosities, from body parts to butterflies, and even public executions. Audiences watched staged fights between animals, whether cockerels in the street or bears and bulls in the royal palaces.

Religious persecution and the Declaration of Rights

Quakers were Christians who said they did not need priests to help them worship God because everyone was equal. They were fined and imprisoned for practising their religion, and between 1662 and 1700 many left Wales to live in a region now known as Pennsylvania in America.

In Scotland, from 1660, Presbyterians were tortured and killed in their thousands during a period known as "The Killing Time". Presbyterians were Protestants who believed that elected elders, instead of appointed bishops, should run the church.

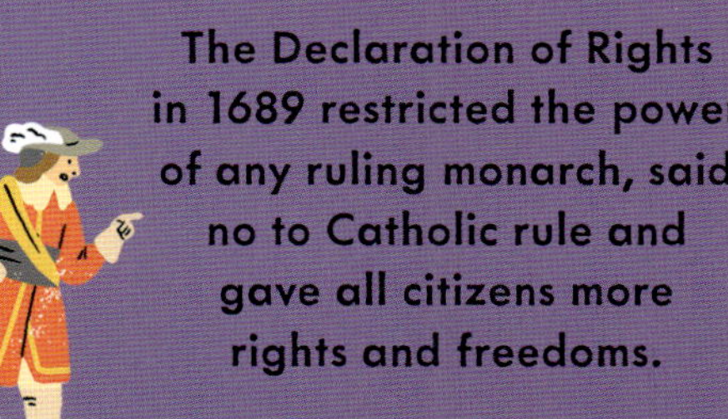

The Declaration of Rights in 1689 restricted the power of any ruling monarch, said no to Catholic rule and gave all citizens more rights and freedoms.

Battle of the Boyne

In 1690, in Ireland, the Protestant King William III defeated the Catholic King James II. The Twelfth of July parades are annual events held in Northern Ireland on 12 July, which is the anniversary of the battle.

Amazing art

Over the centuries, world-famous painters, sculptors and photographers have been inspired by the people and places of the UK. Many artists have developed new styles in response to the changing world around them.

Portrait artists

Some of the earliest professional artists in Britain worked as portrait painters for the rich. Before the seventeenth century, only royals and aristocrats (wealthy people of the upper class who hold land and titles) could afford to have their pictures painted. Later, society changed, and a wealthy middle class made up of doctors, merchants, lawyers and other successful professionals emerged. They were able to pay for portraits, too.

Englishwoman Mary Beale was one of the first women to work as a professional artist. At the peak of her career in 1677, she painted 83 portraits in one year!

Other portrait artists, including William Hogarth, Allan Ramsay, Joshua Reynolds, Thomas Gainsborough and Henry Raeburn, became well known during this period, too.

The Romantics

In the 1800s, many artists began to explore the relationship between nature, poetry and art. This movement, known as "Romanticism", produced artists including landscape painters John Constable and J. M. W. Turner. These two great English artists weren't on the best of terms. It's rumoured that Constable once said, "Turner's pictures are only fit to be spit upon!"

The Pre-Raphaelites

The Pre-Raphaelites were a group of artists who filled their work with drama and spectacle. Their lives were also dramatic – filled with broken hearts and scandals! Their art was influenced by classical literature, religion and the beauty of the natural world. They often painted detailed backgrounds, and subjects with long flowing hair and sumptuous clothes.

Arts and Crafts

By the mid nineteenth century, factories and production lines had made the UK very wealthy, but some artists felt that the industrial age had made everything look boring and plain. The Arts and Crafts movement used good quality materials to create intricate, unique designs, often inspired by nature.

Pop art

The pop art movement spread across the UK in the 1950s. Using bright colours and unique printing techniques, artists such as David Hockney created bold, striking images of everyday objects and events.

British Black Arts movement

In the 1980s, a group of Black artists began a movement challenging the lack of diversity in British art. Through their work, they explored what Black art was, and what it could become in the future. Lubaina Himid and Sonia Boyce used their art to showcase the lives of marginalized communities and paved the way for female Black artists in Britain.

Street art

He may be the most famous street artist in the world, but Banksy has managed to stay anonymous – no one knows who he really is! He started off creating street art in his home city of Bristol in the 1990s. Today, his artwork sells for millions of pounds at auction.

The Turner Prize

This annual award, given to a British artist, is organized by the Tate art galleries. In 1998, Chris Ofili became the first Black artist to win the Turner Prize. He created some of his art out of a very peculiar material – elephant dung!

1660

1790

Trading and uprising

In the early 1660s, Scotland failed to establish an American colony of its own, leading to the union of England and Scotland. There were struggles over the right to trade, the right to rule and the right to own land. The population became urbanized and more people became literate.

England and Scotland unite

The Company of Scotland was formed in 1695. Merchants in Scotland could now legally enslave people and trade goods around the world. In the 1690s, a terrible famine struck. Scottish investors then lost a fortune after the failure of a scheme to create a colony in Panama, in the region now called Central America. England offered to help Scotland, provided they unite as one nation. These terms were agreed, and the Acts of Union merged the parliaments of England and Scotland in 1707.

The Jacobite rebellions

The Jacobites were Scots who wanted the Stuart family of King James II to rule instead of the Hanoverian (German) King George I. England hoped that the Acts of Union would put an end to this rebellion, but in 1715 the Jacobites revolted in the first of many uprisings.

In 1745, a young Stuart prince, Charles Edward, known as "Bonnie Prince Charlie", made another bid for the throne. In 1746, he led a Jacobite army of 6,000 into the Battle of Culloden in the Scottish Highlands. The 9,000 British Army troops, led by the Duke of Cumberland (son of King George II), won the bloody battle.

The British Army terrorized, killed or forced abroad many Highlanders, the people who traditionally lived in the highlands of Scotland. The symbols of Highland culture – wearing tartan, speaking Gaelic and playing the bagpipes – were all banned.

The Penal Laws

In Ireland, "Penal Laws" were enacted in the late seventeenth and early eighteenth centuries, to impose legal restrictions on Catholics. Catholics were forbidden to sit in Parliament or have the vote.

Enclosure

From the 1750s, more and more people lost their rights to farm and graze animals on common land across all four nations. Areas of land were fenced – or "enclosed" – and legally owned by just a few landlords.

Many "commoners" fought back, but they often failed and were forced to rent land or work in factories in the towns. The new owners produced more food, but many people lost their homes and independence.

The Scottish Enlightenment

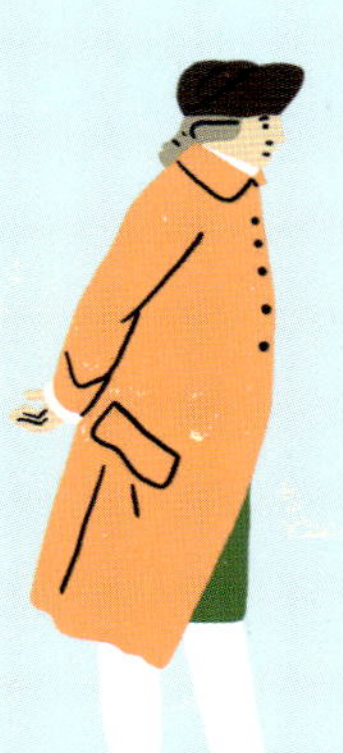

From around 1700 to 1820, Scotland became an important centre for new ideas. Thinkers challenged religious authority and used evidence to develop science. During this time, known as the Enlightenment period, thinkers in the universities shared and discussed their exciting ideas.

They believed that people should have more rights and the freedom to think for themselves. Francis Hutcheson, one of the founders of the Scottish Enlightenment, was strongly against slavery. However, most believed that only men of European descent (like themselves) were deserving of the same rights and freedoms.

The Highland Clearances

In Scotland between 1750 and 1850, Highland communities were evicted from their homes by landowners and their houses were burned down to prevent them from ever returning. The landowners could get more money from sheep and cattle farming than the rent from Highlanders. Over the course of a century, over 100,000 people were left homeless and forced to leave the country.
The Highland Clearances destroyed the traditional clan-based society – which had existed for centuries.

A legacy of literacy

Griffith Jones was a Welsh priest who developed a roving fast-track reading school that could teach someone to read in just three months. When Jones died in 1761, he'd helped establish 3,495 schools in just 30 years. By 1771, 33 per cent of the population of Wales could read in the Welsh language – one of the highest rates of literacy in Europe at the time.

Enslavement and resistance

The brutal system of slavery brought great wealth to the UK for over two hundred years. Enslavement was made illegal in some places in 1834, but Britain continued to profit from investments in slave societies until 1888.

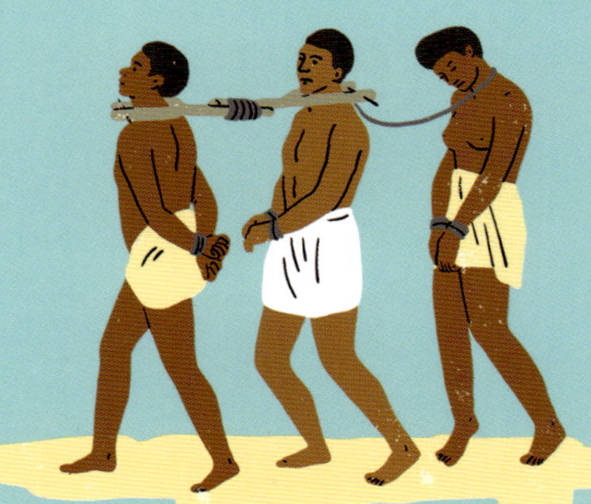

There have been systems of slavery all over the world for centuries. Enslavers take away the freedom of enslaved people and force them to work for free.

The British used slave labour on the North American mainland from 1607 and in the Caribbean from 1623. They killed most of the original peoples of the Caribbean and took their land to farm tropical crops to be sold for profit. Irish and Scottish people who owed money were transported to work on plantations for a few years on an indenture (contract) and freed once they paid their debt. To profit more quickly, the British enslaved millions of people from the continent of Africa to work on the plantations for free.

Chattel slavery

The 1661 Slave Codes of Barbados started the appallingly brutal system of "chattel slavery", meaning enslaved people were fully owned by someone else. They could be bought and sold like property, and any children born to the enslaved women were automatically enslaved, too.

Some African kings and merchants sold people from other African nations who were prisoners of war or accused of petty crimes. Many enslaved people were experts in farming, medicine and industrial crafts. From the sixteenth to the nineteenth century, more than twelve million African people were kidnapped and transported to the Americas.

Over three million people, including children, were taken on British ships. Twenty per cent of the captives sadly died on the two-month journey.

The enslaved people were forced to farm crops, such as tobacco, cotton and sugar, that were sold across the British Empire, making huge profits for plantation owners and merchants. British businesses supplied plantations with goods, such as linen for clothing and fish from Scotland and Northern Ireland.

Enslavers and overseers restricted the workers to terrible food, clothing and lodging. Many people died of extreme overwork and disease just a few years after arrival.

Fighting back

In the Caribbean at this time, there was a constant state of tension and war. Enslaved people would carry out every day acts of resistance in order to rebel, such as breaking machinery or poisoning their enslavers.

African people strategically fought and freed themselves from French enslavers in the Haitian Revolution (1791–1804) in Saint-Domingue (Haiti). They beat the huge British Army sent to re-enslave the people between 1793 and 1798.

In 1722 and 1795, Joseph Chatoyer led two wars of resistance in Saint Vincent. And in 1816, an enslaved man named Bussa led the largest slave revolt in the history of Barbados.

Maroon communities

People in the Caribbean who gained freedom by escaping enslavement established free villages, known as maroon communities.

Queen Nanny in Jamaica is known for setting up the Windward Maroons.

Abolitionists

In Britain, activists and some Members of Parliament fought to abolish the slave trade and enslavement. They were known as "abolitionists". The Society for Effecting the Abolition of the Slave Trade was formed in 1787, headed by Thomas Clarkson and Granville Sharp. In 1807, after a huge campaign by William Wilberforce, Parliament legally abolished the slave trade.

In the 1820s, British women were very active in the abolition movement. Many, like Elizabeth Heyrick, called for people to stop eating sugar grown by enslaved people and to end enslavement immediately.

The Baptist War in Jamaica, in 1831, was an eleven-day revolt involving 60,000 enslaved people. This rebellion helped to push Great Britain to free their slaves in the British Caribbean.

Black abolitionists formed a group called the "Sons of Africa". Olaudah Equiano (see page 34) and Ottobah Cugoano wrote books about their experiences and why slavery was wrong.

Abolition

Britain abolished the slave trade on British ships in 1807, but illegal trafficking continued.

Enslavement in British colonies legally ended on 1 August 1834, and former enslavers received payouts of £20 million. Those enslaved, however, did not receive any compensation for their enslavement.

After abolition, those who had been enslaved were forced to work unpaid for 45 hours a week in the "apprenticeship system". This lasted until 1838. Indentured workers from India were brought to the Caribbean to compensate for the loss of enslaved labour.

Brilliant buildings

From towering clock towers to gravity-defying bridges, the UK is home to some of the world's most impressive buildings and landmarks. Some smaller, simpler structures have fascinating stories to tell, too.

Quay House
Wales

Built in the sixteenth century, Quay House in Conwy is just 3 metres high, 1.8 metres wide and 3 metres deep, making it the smallest house in Britain. The last person to live there was a man named Robert Jones, who was a towering 1.9 metres tall!

Muckle Flugga
Scotland

On the edge of the Island of Unst perches Britain's most northerly lighthouse. It was built in 1854 by brothers Thomas and David Stevenson – the father and uncle of writer Robert Louis Stevenson, author of *Treasure Island*.

The O2 Arena
England

Back in 2000, cities all over the world put on special events to commemorate the start of the new millennium. In London, the iconic Millennium Dome was built to house a special exhibition. The fabric roof spans 365 metres, each metre representing a day in the year! In 2005, the structure was transformed into one of the world's leading live-music venues.

Queen's University
Northern Ireland

In Belfast, the Lanyon Building at Queen's University has been used on banknotes and tourist posters and was named after the man who designed it. Architect Charles Lanyon was inspired by the medieval great halls found at the universities of Oxford and Cambridge.

Forth Bridge
Scotland

More than 4,500 workers were needed to build this monumental Scottish bridge, and sadly several lost their lives during its construction, which occurred between 1882 and 1889. It took over 240,000 litres of red paint to cover the structure.

Grand Opera House
Northern Ireland

Opened in December 1895, this flamboyant theatre was designed so it could be transformed into a circus within 24 hours. It was damaged by bombing in the 1990s but has since been restored to its former glory.

Amazing architects

Behind every great structure is an architect who dreamed it up, and the UK boasts some of the best!

Christopher Wren
1632–1723

After the Fire of London in 1666 (see page 40), much of the English capital was destroyed, including the medieval St Paul's Cathedral. An English architect named Christopher Wren was given the job of designing a new one. It took ten years to plan and almost four times as long to build, but the impressive domed church is now one of the most famous landmarks in London.

Isambard Kingdom Brunel
1806–1859

Victorian engineer Isambard Kingdom Brunel designed many impressive structures during Britain's Industrial Revolution, including the Clifton Suspension Bridge in Bristol and the network of tunnels and bridges that spans the length of the Great Western Railway route.

Zaha Hadid
1950–2016

Iraqi-British architect Zaha Hadid created many interesting buildings around the world in the late twentieth century. Her architectural designs often feel quite futuristic, with sweeping, curved sides made from industrial materials like concrete and steel. In the UK, her buildings include the London Aquatics Centre and Glasgow's Riverside Museum.

Clough Williams-Ellis
1883–1978

Welsh architect Clough Williams-Ellis wanted to prove that a naturally beautiful landscape could be developed without spoiling it. The result, built between 1925 and 1973, was Portmeirion, a picturesque village in Wales that slopes down to the River Dwyryd.

The Industrial Revolution

Inventions created during the Industrial Revolution dramatically changed the state of the economy and society in Britain and Northern Ireland. Many people migrated from the countryside to work in factories in the cities. New infrastructure, such as roads, canals and railways, made transport easier and faster.

Energy sources

Power from wind, water and horses was replaced by power from steam and coal. In 1765, Scottish inventor James Watt made steam-driven piston engines more efficient, so that they could be used to mine coal. Steam was also used to power locomotives, ships and mills. Coal could now be used to power the iron industry.

Innovative inventions

Many British inventions made manufacturing quicker and cheaper. James Hargreaves' spinning jenny and Richard Arkwright's water frame allowed more cotton to be spun faster in order to produce great lengths of fabrics. In the 1780s, Edmund Cartwright's power loom used water power to produce cotton cloth in huge quantities.

Children from as young as four worked down the mines and in the factories. Cruel employers made them work very long hours in very dangerous jobs.

Enclosures of land (see page 45) forced many people to find work in factories. Often, they could not afford to buy basic goods, such as bread. In the "revolt of the housewives" in 1795, women took flour hoarded by merchants and shared it at fair prices with the poor.

New state-of-the-art canals were built in 1731 in County Down, Northern Ireland, and in 1761 in England. Between 1745 and 1830, 4,000 miles of canals were constructed. The coal that powered the factories could now be transported on barges pulled by horses.

Growth of cities

Belfast became Ireland's biggest city during this time. The linen cloth that workers produced from flax was in demand, and villages sprang up around the mills. Many women and children worked in the damp and dusty mills, in bare feet and wet clothes.

George Stephenson, a former mine worker from Northumberland in England, built the first public intercity rail line in the world, which opened in 1830. It used his famous "Rocket" engine and transported raw cotton, grown by enslaved people in the Americas, from the port of Liverpool to Manchester.

In 1804, the very first steam-powered locomotive, invented by Richard Trevithick, hauled 10 tons of iron and 70 men along a track in South Wales.

In 1845, there were over 200,000 "navvies" in the UK, a third of them Irish. They built the railways and used gunpowder to blow out the rock to create tunnels.

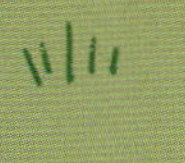

Scotsmen John McAdam and Thomas Telford revolutionized the roads. McAdam's design drained any water, raised the middle and added a crushed-stone surface known as "tarmacadam" or "tarmac". Telford built 920 miles of roads across Scotland and 120 bridges, just for starters.

By 1850, more people in Wales had jobs in industry than agriculture. Much of the coal and iron needed for industry was found in South Wales. There was even a mini gold rush in Dolgellau in the 1850s!

The Luddites were craftsmen who were angry at losing their skilled jobs to new machinery. They wore masks and went on night-time raids to smash and sabotage the new machines.

The British Empire

An empire forms when a person or country rules a group of other countries, or colonies. From the first plantations in North America and Ireland in around 1600, the British Empire spread across the globe to become the biggest empire in the world. At the empire's height in 1922, the British claimed to rule over 458 million people – roughly a quarter of the planet.

North America

After establishing Jamestown, the first British colony in the Americas, in 1607, the British expanded their territory. As well as trafficking African people (see pages 46–47), between 1718 and 1776, under the Transportation Act, over 52,000 convicts were transported to the colonies in America to serve seven to fourteen years of unpaid labour.

Australia

From 1788, Australia became a penal colony (a giant prison) after thousands of people were transported there from Britain, Ireland and British colonies to carry out hard labour. This was punishment for demanding better pay, the right to vote, or for stealing food.

Aboriginal (Indigenous) Australians had been living in Australia for 60,000 years. The British stole land, killed many people and brought deadly diseases. Today, Aboriginal people make up only 3.8 per cent of Australia's population.

Many from Britain and Ireland emigrated to Australia, New Zealand and Canada. Eventually these countries established their own parliaments and governments but they remained linked to the UK and the British crown.

Ireland

The United Irishmen who staged the Irish Rebellion of 1798 wanted independence from Britain. When the revolt failed, the Act of Union in 1801 abolished the Irish Parliament, and Ireland joined with Great Britain to become the United Kingdom.

The Potato Famine

By 1840, the potato was the main food of half the Irish population, but by the late 1840s a disease destroyed most of the potatoes. Other foods such as oats, butter and fish were exported to England as the Irish people starved, resulting in about one million deaths. Relief committees around the world sent food, clothing and money.

Napoleonic Wars

The British competed with other European nations who were also building empires. After a series of wars with France, Britain defeated French leader Napoleon Bonaparte's army at the Battle of Waterloo in 1815. Finally, after 23 years, the Napoleonic Wars came to an end and the British Empire expanded even further.

Colonial control

The British Empire took resources, such as metals or precious stones, from their colonies and imposed taxes on the people living there.

The British often forced people to give up their religions and cultures, in order to become Christians and to speak English.

New borders separated communities and sometimes led to wars.

At times the British struggled to keep their control as other nations fought back. The First War of Independence fought in India in 1857 and the victory by the Zulu nation at the Battle of Isandlwana in 1879 shocked the British.

When some British administrators refused to carry out orders that would harm local people, they were sent back to Britain. Famous British people like artist William Morris and writer Thomas Hardy also spoke out against the violence of the British Empire.

At the Berlin Conference in Germany (1884–1885), fourteen European leaders divided up the continent of Africa between themselves. They agreed to let each other take the rich resources of Africa without asking any Africans. Britain took 20 of these new colonies.

Boer Wars

In the Boer Wars in South Africa (1899–1902), thousands of Boer (Dutch-descended) and African people died in British concentration camps. Controlling the mining of diamonds and gold in South Africa brought great wealth to Britain.

The Boy Scout movement was set up in 1908 and Girl Guides in 1910 to prepare British youth for defending the British Empire. Today, there are more than 31 million scouts across the world.

As a result of the British Empire, English is a widely spoken language, allowing communication across continents.

End of the empire

1765

Present

Over time, the British Empire began to break apart in a process called "decolonization". Decolonization is the gradual process of colonies gaining independence. After World War II, decolonization sped up dramatically, leaving behind a network of former British colonies called the Commonwealth.

THE BRITISH EMPIRE

The success of the American Revolution (1775–1783) led to the United States becoming the first nation to gain independence from Britain.

In the 1890s, people at home and abroad called for various colonies to be independent. Writers such as Celestine Edwards and Catherine Impey, as well as the magazines *Lux and Fraternity*, used their publications to promote anti-imperialist beliefs.

Countries with populations of majority European descent were given dominion status first: Canada in 1867, Australia in 1901 and South Africa in 1910. However, the colonies in Africa and the Caribbean were never given dominion status.

The UK became a meeting place for people of African descent from all over the world. Henry Sylvester Williams organised the first Pan-African conference in 1900, calling for better rights for people of African descent.

By granting colonies independence, the UK could still profit from cheap labour and cheap resources from ex-colonies without the expense of running them directly. Many ex-colonies now pay more in interest to world banks and former colonizing countries than they receive in aid.

After decolonization, the British Government destroyed and hid thousands of documents about the colonies. Politicians were particularly keen to hide the truth about the concentration camps they ran in Kenya in the 1950s.

In 1922, after a war of independence, the area of southern Ireland broke away from the UK and became an independent state. Northern Ireland opted to stay in the UK.

In 1947, India gained its independence from Britain in return for fighting during World War II. When the British withdrew from India, they divided it into two separate countries, Hindu-majority India and Muslim-majority Pakistan.

Two million people died in the violent separation, and families were split up as fifteen million people were forced to move.

Japan invaded British-ruled Malaya during World War II. When the Communist Party of Malaya fought for self-rule, the British brought in soldiers from other countries and rounded up Chinese Malaysians into prison camps. Malaya finally became an independent country called Malaysia in 1957.

The first country in Africa to declare independence was Ghana in West Africa under president Kwame Nkrumah in 1957. Many other African countries followed suit.

South Africa's system of apartheid (apartness), which discriminated against the Black and Asian majority, began developing in the early 1900s and did not end until 1994.

Map not to scale. Accurate to 1901.

The Commonwealth

In 1926, the first countries were invited to join the UK in a new network of countries called the British Commonwealth, which formed in 1931.

The Commonwealth today is made up of a network of 56 countries across the world. Most are ex-British colonies, comprising 2.5 billion people (roughly a third of the world population). Most states are republics with a president, but fifteen retain the British monarch as their head of state, including Australia and Canada. The Commonwealth allows networking across nations and access to scholarships to study in the UK.

There are fourteen British overseas territories that remain part of the British Empire.

Sensational sport

Many of the sports we play across the UK today have a long history. Rules have changed and teams have come and gone, but the British competitive spirit remains!

Darts

Darts began as a game played in pubs across the UK. Formal rules were put in place shortly after World War I. In the 1930s, several areas banned the sport, including Liverpool and Glasgow, as some authorities worried playing it would encourage drunkenness!

Cricket

Historians think that cricket was invented by children, but by the seventeenth century it was a popular sport for adults, too. It was one of the few games that women were sometimes allowed to play, although they had to wear long dresses, which must have been hard to run in!

Netball

Netball was first played in England in 1895. The rules were based on the new American game of basketball, but through a misunderstanding it was thought that certain players couldn't leave certain areas, and the zones of netball were created.

Polo

A version of polo has been played in Asia for thousands of years. In 1859, British tea planters in India learned the game. The following decade, British Army officers brought it back to the UK.

Football or rugby?

Football was a popular sport in medieval England. A ball would be kicked or tossed across a pitch – which could span a whole town. Rules varied from place to place, and matches could last for days. In Tudor times, laws were passed forbidding football as too many men were getting injured or killed!

It wasn't until the nineteenth century that rugby and football went their separate ways. In 1823, during a game of football at Rugby School in the West Midlands, one of the players picked up the ball . . . and began to run with it. This version of the game soon spread around the UK.

By 1863, the different rules of football and rugby were established and, in 1871, Scotland played England in the very first international rugby game. A few years later, Gaelic football rules, with both rugby and football elements, were also standardized. The sport remains popular in Northern Ireland. Rugby players from Northern Ireland play for the All Ireland team and the British and Irish Lions team.

Badminton

The game of badminton is named after Badminton House, a grand estate in England. In 1863, the Duke of Beaufort invited his guests to play a game using shuttlecocks there.

Tennis

King Henry VIII was a keen tennis player, and he had many indoor courts built all over the country. In 1850, new, bouncier tennis balls were invented, which meant the sport could be played on grass outside. In 1877, the first tennis tournament was held at Wimbledon, England. Only men could play, and they had to wear hats, ties and heeled shoes!

Lots of other sports including curling, rounders and hockey were also invented in the UK.

Women's suffrage and World War I

The early twentieth century was a turbulent time in the UK. Women ramped up their fight for equal rights and the right to vote. World War I (1914–1918) was the first war fought by nations across the breadth of the world. Many new technologies were used, such as planes and tanks. When the war ended with a ceasefire (an agreement between enemies to stop fighting) in 1918, Germany was punished. After the war, a terrible flu pandemic took many more lives.

Women's suffrage

Women in Britain had been proposing voting rights from 1792 and petitioning for them since the 1830s. From 1867, the movement gained strength.

The more moderate "suffragists" pushed for support inside Parliament for women's voting rights. The more militant "suffragettes" used direct action, like window-smashing and arson (deliberately starting fires), to draw attention to the cause. Many were jailed and went on hunger strike.

In 1918, after many years of activism, some women (aged over 30 and owning property) gained the right to vote. By 1928, all women had equal voting rights with men from the age of 21.

World War I

On 28 June 1914, Gavrilo Princip assassinated (killed) Archduke Franz Ferdinand and his wife, Sophie, in Sarajevo in Bosnia-Herzegovina.

Princip was a Serbian nationalist who was angry that Austria-Hungary ruled his people. Austria-Hungary declared war, and over 30 countries took sides.

On the side of the Allies were Britain, France, Belgium, Russia and the US. They fought against the Central Powers: Germany, Austria-Hungary, Bulgaria and Turkey.

Women's war effort

Many British women worked in factories making weapons. Although this work was hard and dangerous, they were paid less than men.

Elsie Inglis was a Scottish doctor who set up all-female hospitals across Europe.

Battles of World War I

The Allies and the Central Powers had many battles. Some of the most well-known were the First Battle of the Marne, the battle of Gallipoli and the Battle of the Somme, where 20,000 British troops died on the first day of fighting.

War vehicles

Tanks and planes were used in war for the first time. The Germans swapped their lumbering airships, called Zeppelins, which they used to bomb British cities, for faster long-range heavy bombers. In April 1918, the Royal Air Force (RAF) was formed.

Over 15,000 volunteers from the West Indies (the Caribbean) formed the British West Indies Regiment.

During the Christmas Day truce in 1914, British and German soldiers stopped fighting to bury their dead, exchange gifts and play football.

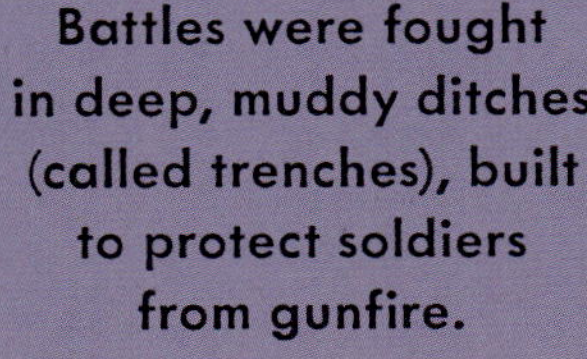

Battles were fought in deep, muddy ditches (called trenches), built to protect soldiers from gunfire.

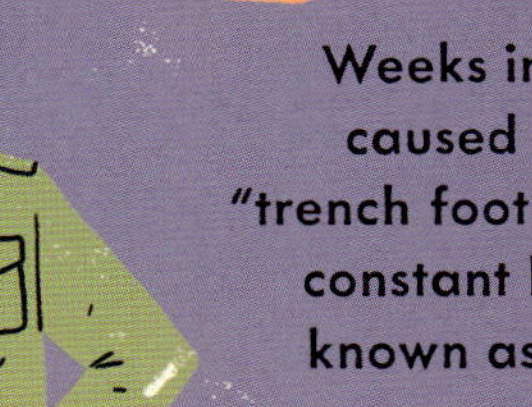

Weeks in the trenches caused diseases like "trench foot", and stress from constant bombardment, known as "shell shock".

Sixteen million out of 65 million soldiers died in World War I. At 11 a.m. on the eleventh day of the eleventh month (November), a two-minute silence is held to remember the time in 1918 when both sides agreed to stop fighting.

At the Treaty of Versailles in 1919, the Allies punished Germany, taking away land on its borders and its colonies, and making the country pay £6.6 billion.

When British soldiers came home, there were not enough jobs. Disgracefully, mobs of white soldiers in many port towns, including Cardiff and Glasgow, took out their frustration by attacking Black and Asian sailors who had fought alongside them.

Flu

From 1918 to 1919, a deadly flu pandemic spread across the world and killed an estimated 50 million people. Three big waves hit the UK in 1918 and 1919, with British soldiers returning from the trenches in France. Sometimes, people died the same day they fell ill. There were no vaccines or antibiotics, so people tried to contain the virus through extra hygiene and isolation.

One of the very few places in the world that wasn't affected was Marajó island in the Amazon River in Brazil.

The 1920s and 1930s

After the devastation of World War I, society continued to change. Northern Ireland was formed as the rest of Ireland became independent (see page 55), and in Britain some women gained more rights and freedoms. After the Great Depression, political ideas such as communism and fascism became popular. In 1939, yet another world war broke out.

World War I was so traumatic that many people vowed it would be the "war to end war", as British author H.G. Wells wrote. From 1925 to 1939, women and children all over Wales held "Daffodil days" to raise money by growing and selling daffodils for world peace.

The new Northern Ireland, established in 1922 (see page 55), consisted of a Protestant majority who were mostly unionist and wanted to maintain the link with Britain, and a large Catholic minority who were mostly nationalist and wanted a united Ireland. Political and violent tensions grew following the Irish War of Independence and led to the loss of many lives, particularly among the Catholic community.

Margaret Bondfield became the first female UK cabinet minister in January 1929.

General Election

Labour candidate

Flappers

In the 1920s, the wealthy enjoyed lavish parties. Women in these social circles became known as "flappers" or "bright young things". They wore short hair and knee-length skirts and began driving, smoking and drinking alcohol – things that shocked society at the time!

Life for children

In 1921, state primary school was free for every child in England and Wales from five to fourteen years old, but many children had to stay at home and look after younger brothers and sisters. Pupils used chalk and a slate, or a stick in the sand, to practise their letters. Punishments included writing lines (copying out the same sentence over and over again) or being hit with a ruler or a cane! The laws were different for schoolchildren in Scotland and Northern Ireland (see page 66).

Childhood diseases, such as rickets, polio and tuberculosis, were very common. Penicillin, a medicine called an "antibiotic", was discovered by Alexander Fleming in 1928. Penicillin cured bacterial infections and saved many lives.

The Great Crash

In 1929, the stock market in the US crashed. Many people had put money into businesses hoping to receive profits, but they lost their money when the businesses failed. Goods leaving the UK were suddenly worth half as much. Unemployment in the UK doubled by the end of 1930, creating much poverty and hardship. In some regions, unemployment was as high as 70 per cent. This catastrophic event was called the "Great Depression".

Fascism and communism

In the 1930s, many people in the UK were interested in having a fascist government. Fascist societies have controlling leaders who can punish people for not obeying the rules. Oswald Mosley was an English fascist supported by a violent gang of "blackshirts".

Between 1935 and 1939, communism became particularly popular as an idea to share wealth equally between people. However, as with Fascist societies, Communist societies at the time had all-powerful leadership and violent punishments for those who disagreed.

Few people had electricity in their homes or an inside toilet. Families enjoyed visiting the seaside, swimming in outdoor pools and cycling. People loved watching films from Hollywood at the cinema, such as the first colour film, *The Wizard of Oz* (1939), and reading paperback books and comics, like the *Beano*.

King Edward VIII fell in love with an American woman named Wallis Simpson. She was divorced, and the Church of England and the government disapproved of their relationship. In 1936, Edward gave up the throne to his younger brother, who was crowned George VI.

Prime Minister Neville Chamberlain did not want to go to war with Germany when it invaded its neighbouring country of Czechoslovakia in 1938. He tried to strike a deal with the German leader Adolf Hitler, called the "policy of appeasement".

World War II

1939
1945

After Germany invaded several countries in Europe, the UK declared war. When Germany began to bomb UK cities, life changed dramatically. Children were sent away from the cities to the countryside, men left for war, and women worked in factories and on farms. The German army and its allies were eventually defeated, but the war took an enormous toll.

1 September 1939

BRITAIN AT WAR!

When the leader of Germany, Adolf Hitler, used an army to invade Poland on 1 September 1939, the UK and France declared war against him. Germany continued to invade other European countries.

World War II lasted from 1939 to 1945. The Allies, including Britain, France, China and the US, fought against the Axis nations, including Germany, Italy and Japan. In all, 1.7 billion people from over 50 countries were involved.

The Nazi government in Germany discriminated against Jewish people, who were in increasing danger. A rescue effort, called the *Kindertransport*, brought 10,000 children from Nazi territories to the safety of foster families in the UK by boat and train in the build-up to the war.

The Blitz

The Blitz was a bombing campaign against towns and cities in the UK that started in September 1940 and continued for eight months until May 1941. London was the worst-affected area, with around 43,000 people killed and one in six Londoners made homeless. Liverpool, Swansea, Glasgow and Belfast were also targets – half of the homes in Belfast were damaged or destroyed during the raids.

People wore gas masks and blacked out their windows so that the German bombers couldn't spot any lights. When enemy planes were spotted, alarms gave civilians a short time to rush to the safety of underground air-raid shelters.

During the Battle of Britain in 1940, the RAF Fighter Command used their superior fighter aircraft to defeat the Luftwaffe (the German air force). The Nazis were furious and began bombing civilians.

Children who lived in cities in danger of being bombed were "evacuated" – sent to stay with foster families in the countryside.

In 1945, the British struck back against the Germans by bombing German targets, including a devastating attack on the city of Dresden, where 25,000 civilians tragically lost their lives.

Life at home

The Women's Land Army replaced male farm workers and women quickly learned how to plough, milk cows and drive tractors. Women worked in factories, too, and in 1942 some became "Lumber Jills" (female lumberjacks).

Children helped the war effort by recycling scrap items, raising money or knitting to cheer up the soldiers. Those aged fourteen to seventeen worked in agriculture or industry, and boys were sent to the army at eighteen.

In Wales, men had to work in the mines instead of fighting. In Northern Ireland, men did not have to fight but many still chose to.

Food was rationed so that everyone had enough to eat. Meat, dairy, eggs and sugar were restricted, so many people, including children, grew vegetables.

The Germans sent submarines (U-boats) across the Atlantic Ocean to blow up Allied ships bringing food from the US and the Caribbean to the UK. The Allies sent convoys to protect them. Losses on both sides in the Battle of the Atlantic were terrible. As many as 70,000 people lost their lives.

More than 110,000 Gurkha soldiers from India and Nepal served in the war.

Some 6,000 Caribbean men volunteered to work for the RAF, and 450 became aircrew, including fighter pilots.

Bletchley Park was a secret centre in England where mathematicians, such as Alan Turing, deciphered the complicated Enigma Code that the Nazis had created to send secret messages. The cracking of this code using state-of-the-art computers and brainpower helped save millions of lives.

The end of the war

On 6 June 1944, known as D-Day, the Allied forces began their invasion of the Normandy coast in France. This strategic event led many Nazis to surrender. Celebrations burst out all over the country when the war finally came to an end – on VE Day (Victory in Europe) on 8 May 1945 and VJ Day (Victory over Japan) on 15 August 1945.

Scientific discoveries and inventions

Today's world would look very different were it not for the important developments and discoveries made by scientists and inventors across the UK. From the telephone to the chocolate bar, the contributions of British brains have changed the course of world history!

Evolution

In his 1859 book *On the Origin of Species*, Charles Darwin provided an explanation for how living things can change and adapt over many generations with his famous theory of evolution. Darwin took taxidermy lessons with a man named John Edmonstone from Guyana in South America. John had been formerly enslaved but was now a successful business owner. As well as teaching Darwin how to preserve dead animals, Edmonstone also taught him about the wildlife of South America.

The telephone

Scottish-born Alexander Graham Bell invented the telephone in 1876 with his assistant Thomas Watson. The first-ever words on a phone call were: "Mr Watson – come here – I want you."

The computer

You might think of computers as a relatively recent invention, but back in the nineteenth century English engineer Charles Babbage and English mathematician Ada Lovelace dreamed up a device called an "Analytical Engine". Although it was never built, the engine was designed to use codes and instructions similar to today's computers.

The chocolate bar

The first solid chocolate bar was invented in Bristol in 1847. Compared to modern chocolatey treats, it was dry, crumbly and not very sweet, but it still became popular.

Ancient fossils

Nineteenth-century fossil hunter Mary Anning lived on the south-west coast of England and spent many hours combing the shore for signs of long-dead creatures. After carefully chiselling these curiosities out of the rock, she would sell them to beachgoers. Mary discovered some impressive fossils, including an ichthyosaur when she was just twelve years old, as well as a plesiosaur and pterosaur.

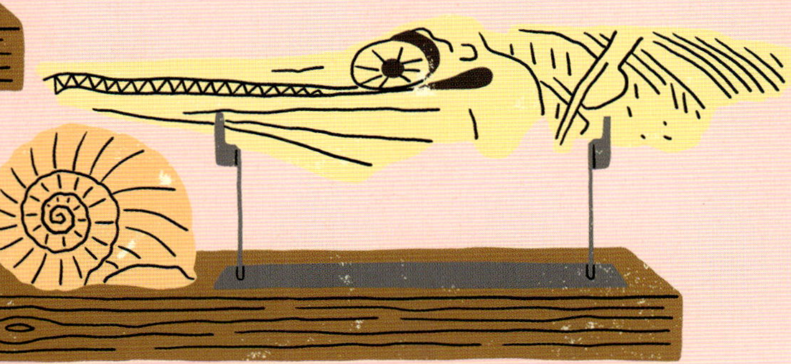

Discoveries in space

In 1967, Jocelyn Bell Burnell discovered pulsars – a type of super-dense star that emits pulsing radio waves as it spins round.

Another British space genius was Stephen Hawking, who, during the twentieth century, showed that black holes emit radiation.

Today, Maggie Aderin-Pocock is a leading space scientist, involved in making equipment for projects like the new James Webb Space Telescope, the world's largest and most powerful space telescope.

Penicillin

After forgetting to wash up some bacteria-covered petri dishes in his laboratory in 1928, Scottish scientist Alexander Fleming noticed the dishes had gone mouldy.

Interestingly, the mould had a bacteria-free halo. Fleming's discovery led to the invention of antibiotics – important drugs that fight off infection and have saved millions of lives.

DNA

During the 1950s, biologists James Watson, from the United States, and Francis Crick, from England, worked together to reveal the structure of our DNA, using X-rays created by English chemist Rosalind Franklin. Their research led to many discoveries and scientific achievements, including the creation of Dolly the sheep, the first-ever cloned mammal to be created from an adult cell.

The television

A far cry from the flatscreen TVs of today, Scottish inventor John Logie Baird's first television was cobbled together from odds and ends, including a bicycle lamp, a hat box and a biscuit tin!

The 1940s and 1950s

1940

1959

After World War II, the UK needed to rebuild. It relied on loans and workers from its colonies to get back on its feet. Universal health, education and welfare for the poor were introduced. In the 1950s, new housing was built to replace the homes that had been destroyed.

The return home

Soldiers fighting across the globe took up to five years to make their way home. Many had been stuck in prison camps and suffered from mental and physical injuries. Men were overjoyed to be back with their families and loved ones after such horrific events.

The last of the 2.5 million children who had been evacuated to the countryside were sent home by train. They were happy to be home and safe again, but were often sad to leave their foster families. Sometimes, they didn't recognize their original families or homes.

Families expanded with a "baby boom" in the years after the war – 900,000 babies were born in the UK in 1946.

Recovery from war

The UK was in debt totalling £3 billion after the war. The government forced people in India to pay £100 million in taxes. They also sent the British Army to some colonies to make them sell their resources to the UK at very cheap prices. They used this money to pay back some of their debts and to help rebuild the country.

The Education Acts of 1944 in England and Wales, and 1945 in Scotland, brought free schooling to everyone. In 1947 in Northern Ireland, The Education Act allowed more Catholics to go to school and have equal opportunities.

The Windrush generation

People from the Caribbean began to arrive in the UK on ships, such as the SS *Ormonde* and *Almanzora* in 1947, the *Windrush* in 1948 and *Georgic* in 1949. Many of the men had served Britain in the RAF and were returning to study, train and work as there was no work at home.

In 1948, the Irish government turned their 26 counties into a republic. The British government left it up to the Stormont government in Northern Ireland to decide if they wanted to stop being part of the UK. They chose to stay.

Elizabeth II became queen in February 1952 at the age of 25, when she got the news that her father King George VI had died. Her coronation at Westminster Abbey in 1953 was the first ever to be on TV. Northern Ireland got a TV transmitter for the very first time so that people could watch it.

Rebuilding the UK

In 1946, there were 402,000 German prisoners of war stuck in the UK who were forced to repair roads, make bricks and work in construction. Thousands of Germans who stayed and became British citizens had been Nazis.

Almost four million homes had been destroyed in the war. In the 1950s, 2.5 million houses were built, many in brand-new towns. The first was Stevenage in Hertfordshire, with ten more by 1955. Huge areas of slum housing were demolished, and people moved from their communities to live in new, tall blocks of flats. There was so much work to do that there weren't enough workers!

The NHS

The National Health Service (NHS) was set up by Aneurin Bevan in 1948, granting free healthcare to everyone in the UK. The government recruited workers from sixteen colonies and ex-colonies. By 1954, 3,000 NHS nurses were from the Caribbean, and by the end of the 1950s, up to 40 per cent of all junior doctors were from South Asia.

The 1960s and 1970s

With more freedom and money to spend in the 1960s, young people created their own teenage tribes. But, as the economy slumped in the 1970s, the UK suffered from yet more unemployment and strikes.

The Swinging Sixties

In the 1960s, London became the epicentre of "cool". Teenagers enjoyed a new sense of freedom. Food rationing and army conscription had ended, there were more places at colleges and universities, more jobs to go around, and there was more money to spend.

As fashion became more affordable, groups of youth "tribes" emerged with their own distinct dress senses and social codes.

Supermarkets, colour TV and transistor radios all became popular.

The last execution in the UK happened in 1964.

WOMEN UNITE

The women's liberation movement began, demanding women have the same rights as men, such as equal pay. Some women began to wear miniskirts and trousers for the first time. By 1964, women could finally legally own their own money and property.

In 1966, England hosted the Football World Cup . . . and won! Over half the population of Britain watched the final on TV.

The struggle for racial equality

In 1962 and 1968, laws were passed to limit Black and Asian immigration. In 1968, Member of Parliament Enoch Powell made an infamous speech whipping up fears of immigration, even though he had recruited nurses from the Caribbean for the NHS.

The Bristol Bus Boycott of 1963 was a historic victory, which forced a local bus company to employ Black and Asian drivers and conductors.

The Race Relations Acts of 1965 and 1968 began to outlaw racial discrimination.

The Striking Seventies

In the 1970s, wages were low and unemployment was rising. Many workers went on strike to demand better pay and working conditions.

The Grunwick dispute in London (1976–1978) was led by South Asian women protesting against the awful conditions in their factory. Over 500 people were arrested before they were forced to stop their protest.

Most of the UK's energy came from coal and oil. During the coal miners' strike of 1972, the government limited the working week to three days to save electricity. Oil from the Middle East shot up in price in 1973, making things even more expensive.

The Troubles

In Northern Ireland, during the period known as "The Troubles", from 1968 to 1998, a total of 3,635 people lost their lives due to political violence. In June 2010, then prime minister David Cameron apologized for the unjustified killings on a tragic day known as Bloody Sunday (30 January 1972), when the British Army shot dead thirteen unarmed men and boys, and injured fourteen more.

People power

Facing racism in housing, work and school, people from the Caribbean started the British Black Panther movement and organized "Saturday schools" for children, teaching subjects including history and politics.

Black and white people united through music. From 1976, punk and reggae bands held concerts to "Rock Against Racism".

The Winter of Discontent

The freezing winter of 1978–1979 had terrible storms and 47 centimetres of snowfall! More workers went on strike, including gravediggers in Liverpool. Dead bodies and rubbish piled up, and the NHS only accepted emergencies.

The personal computer was invented in 1971. The mobile phone, invented in 1973, was as big as a brick!

Wales campaigned for the BBC to broadcast Welsh radio and TV shows. They graffitied English place-name signs with Welsh names and threatened hunger strikes to get their needs met.

In May 1979, Margaret Thatcher, the UK's first female prime minister, came to power.

Magnificent music

Long before the invention of records and radios, music was an important part of life in the UK. Traditional songs were played at dances and gatherings, the melodies handed down from generation to generation. Today, UK artists create an immense variety of music.

New sounds

From heavy metal to indie rock, grime to techno, UK artists invented, developed and made popular lots of new genres over the decades following the 1960s. Many musicians became legends, and their impact can still be felt all over the world. A lot of modern music merges different styles together, with popular artists such as Ed Sheeran mixing genres of folk, rock and pop.

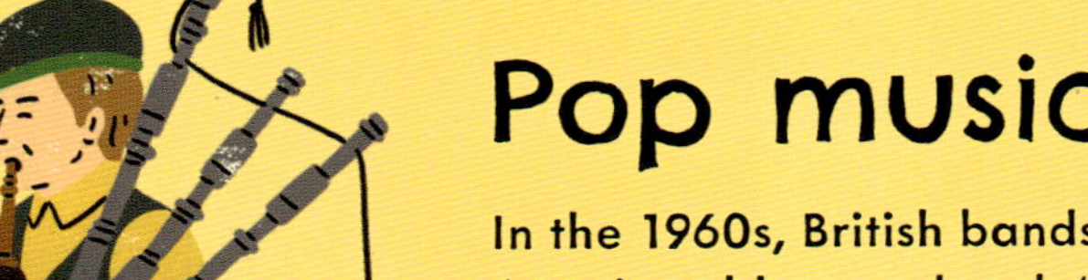

Pop music

In the 1960s, British bands inspired by American blues and rock 'n' roll began to create their own distinct pop music style. The catchy songs of artists like the Beatles and the Rolling Stones became so famous in the United States that the press labelled their popularity a "British invasion".

Bagpipes

Most people think of bagpipes as a Scottish invention, but the iconic instrument likely comes from North Africa. Historians think they were brought to Britain by the Romans. Traditionally made from animal skin, the bag part is inflated by a piper blowing into the mouthpiece.

Welsh choirs

Wales is known as the "Land of Song", and male voice choirs are a big part of the reason why. During the economic depression of the 1920s and 1930s, many miners found themselves out of work. Choirs were a way to pass the time, and they gave people a sense of purpose.

UK record-breakers

Discover a few UK performers who have smashed records with their music!

Britpop band Oasis's hit "All Around the World" was the longest song to ever top the UK charts when it made number one in 1998.

It lasts a whopping nine minutes and thirty-eight seconds!

The first grime album to reach number one in the UK charts was Stormzy's *Gang Signs and Prayer* in 2017.

The fastest-selling single in UK history is "Candle in the Wind" by Elton John.

Scottish-Northern Irish band Snow Patrol's song "Chasing Cars" spent a record 166 weeks in the UK charts.

London-born Adele was the first female singer in history to have three top-ten singles in the charts at the same time.

When promoting his third album, Ed Sheeran broke the record for the most tickets sold for a concert tour.

A total of 8,882,182 fans turned up to watch his 255 shows, which took place across six continents.

The Spice Girls have the most number-one hits of any girl band, taking the top spot an incredible nine times.

1980
1999

The 1980s and 1990s

The 1980s were a time of big fashion, big concerts and a big storm. The UK went to war with Argentina but saw the rise of the peace movement. The 1990s brought poll-tax riots, grief over the death of Princess Diana and peace in Northern Ireland.

Pop culture

The Live Aid concert at Wembley Stadium in 1985 was a sixteen-hour fundraising show for famine relief in Ethiopia. More than 75 British musical acts were watched on television by nearly two billion people worldwide!

Fashion was all about big hair, big shoulders and bright colours in the 1980s. Kids enjoyed writing to pen pals, going to roller discos and solving a Rubik's Cube puzzle.

Music videos were new and exciting. In 1983, Michael Jackson released a mini film for his song "Thriller" that lasted thirteen minutes!

War and peace

The Falklands War

In 1982, the Falklands War was fought over the rights to the Falkland Islands off the coast of Argentina in South America. Britain had seized the islands in 1833, and Argentina wanted them back. The UK dispatched 20 warships, and Argentinian forces surrendered ten weeks later.

Greenham Common Women's Peace Camp

A Women's Peace Camp began in 1981 outside Greenham Common airbase in Berkshire, England, protesting the 96 nuclear missiles due to be stored there. Supporters came from all over the world. By 1991, all of these missiles had been sent back to the US.

Nuclear Disarmament

By 1983, the Campaign for Nuclear Disarmament had become the largest peace movement in the world, with 340,000 UK members. They hope to get rid of nuclear weapons for good.

Earth, wind and fire

A great storm ripped through the UK in 1987. Wind gusts of 100 miles per hour took down fifteen million trees, killed eighteen people and cut off power for 24 hours.

From 1979 to 1991, there were 228 mysterious arson attacks on holiday homes in Wales owned by English people. The culprits were never found.

The 1980s saw the gap grow between the rich and poor, and the north and south of the UK. Miners went on strike (1984–1985) but the government had secretly stockpiled the coal the country needed.

In 1981, there were uprisings in urban Black communities across England protesting racism, unemployment and police harassment.

In 1990, the poll-tax riots erupted over an unfair tax. Poor people were told to pay the same for local services as millionaires. After violent protests, a fairer council tax was introduced.

The Channel Tunnel opened in 1994, allowing people to travel from England to France in a vehicle underneath the sea. In 1990, the British tunnel workers met the French tunnel workers in the middle, and they drank champagne together!

Englishman Tim Berners-Lee invented the World Wide Web in 1989.

Princess Diana and Prince Charles (Queen Elizabeth II's eldest son) had a fairy-tale royal wedding in 1981. When Princess Diana died in a car crash in Paris in 1997, fans in the UK laid down bouquets of flowers and lit candles.

In 1998, the Good Friday Agreement ended most of the conflict and violence in Northern Ireland. The Agreement created the Northern Ireland Assembly and allowed different political parties to share power.

A new century

The 2000s began with fears over a new millennium, took the UK into new wars and introduced new toys. Royal celebrations and sporting events excited the nation, while votes divided opinion on whether countries should leave the UK or Europe. Increasing digital connections encouraged "viral" videos and the rise of the UK gaming industry.

In the run up to the year 2000, people feared that, as the new millennium (thousand years) began, the clocks would not recognize the time and all the computers would crash! This threat was referred to as the "millennium bug".

The UK's biggest demonstration ever was against the invasion of Iraq in 2003. An estimated two million people protested in London and 61,000 in Glasgow. The war went ahead anyway.

The UK gained a reputation for developing cool games and swiftly became the biggest gaming industry in Europe. With advances in technology, the Xbox, Nintendo DS and Nintendo Wii filled people's homes. Netflix began its film service in 1998 by posting DVDs for hire!

Sporting events

The Olympics

London hosted the Olympic Games in the summer of 2012. The spectacular opening ceremony included Queen Elizabeth II, James Bond (played by actor Daniel Craig) and a celebration of the NHS. The Great Britain and Northern Ireland Olympic Team won 65 medals – the most in over a century!

In 2013, Andy Murray, from Dunblane in Scotland, became the first British man to win the men's tennis finals at Wimbledon since 1936.

Glasgow hosted the Commonwealth Games in 2014, the largest event Scotland had ever held.

Leicester City shocked the country by winning the English Premier League in 2016. This was the first win for the team in their 132-year history!

Saying "I do"

Prince Harry (the son of King Charles III and the late Princess Diana) married Meghan Markle, an American actor, in a spectacular royal wedding at Windsor Castle in 2018. Meghan's veil was nearly 5 metres long and embroidered with the national flowers of 53 Commonwealth countries!

In 2014, same-sex marriage was made legal in most of the UK. This meant that two men or two women could marry each other. Northern Ireland followed suit in 2020.

Yes or no? To stay or go?

Brexit vote

Brexit is a short name for "British Exit". The European Union (EU) is a club of 27 European countries (28 including the UK) formed so that citizens can move freely and trade goods in exchange for following certain rules. In 2016, just over half (52 per cent) of the UK population voted to leave the EU to have more control over national decisions. The UK finally left on 31 December 2020. Unlike in England and Wales, most people in Scotland and Northern Ireland voted to stay in the EU.

The Scottish independence referendum

In 2014, people aged sixteen and over in Scotland voted in a referendum (a chance to say "yes" or "no" on a big decision) on whether or not Scotland should become an independent country. The majority chose to stay in the UK, with 55 per cent voting against independence.

Grenfell Tower

A devastating fire destroyed the 24-storey Grenfell Tower in London in 2017. The exterior covering was dangerously flammable and there were no sprinklers. Once the fire started, some residents were told to stay in their flats. The fire brigade, other emergency workers and local residents tried their best to get everyone to safety, but sadly 72 people died.

Queen Elizabeth II's diamond jubilee in 2012 celebrated 60 years of her reign. The Queen and her husband, Prince Philip, toured the country and hosted a cavalcade (a procession with horses and carriages) at Windsor Castle.

2020

Present

The modern day

The Covid-19 virus changed our lives. Lockdowns prevented people from going to work or school. The Black Lives Matter movement came into focus after the murder of George Floyd. Brexit has already brought big changes, but who knows what else the future will bring?

Covid-19

The Covid-19 virus first appeared in Wuhan, China, and spread rapidly across the world from January 2020. When scientists discovered that the virus spreads through the air, people kept their distance and wore masks. Many people died, but the vaccines that were developed in the UK were a great success. People and communities banded together to help one another.

Being made to stay at home during several "lockdowns" sparked big changes in lifestyle and learning. People started communicating digitally, over video calls, for work and school. Many people took up new hobbies, such as baking and caring for new pets. Online food deliveries became popular when people were not able to go to shops or restaurants.

Black Lives Matter

In June 2020, the Black Lives Matter (BLM) movement suddenly entered the spotlight around the world when American police killed a man called George Floyd. BLM is a movement for civil rights that started in the US to highlight the murders of Black people and to protest against racial discrimination. People in the UK protested to highlight similar problems.

Many people in the city of Bristol had been complaining for years about a statue of Edward Colston. He had trafficked many people, including children, into enslavement in the Caribbean. In the summer of 2020, a crowd of young people pulled the statue down and threw it into the docks.

Brexit

The UK finally left the European Union (Brexit) on 31 December 2020, after many negotiations and agreements. In 2022, as families tried to go on holidays abroad again after Covid-19, there was a great deal of travel chaos on the roads and at airports. In April 2022, a queue of 2,000 lorries stretched 20 miles back from the port of Dover in Kent, England.

British Sign Language Act

British Sign Language (BSL) is the most commonly used sign language in the UK. In April 2022, BSL became legally recognized as an official language in the UK.

Rising temperatures

COP26, the twenty-sixth "Conference of Parties", was held in Glasgow, Scotland, in November 2021. More than 200 world leaders met to try to work together to prevent the Earth from getting too hot. In the UK, temperatures in the summer of 2022 hit a new high of 40 degrees Celsius.

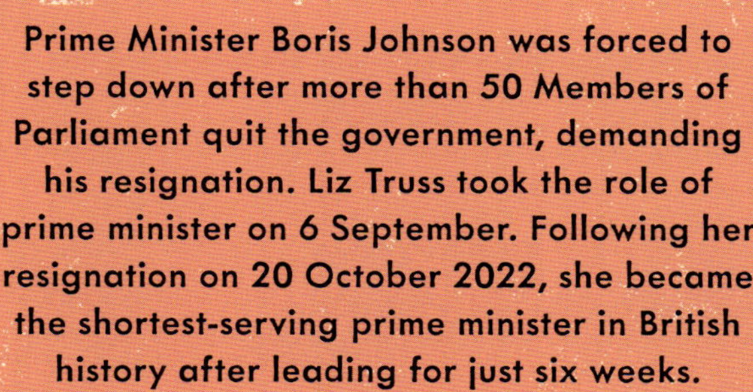

Prime Minister Boris Johnson was forced to step down after more than 50 Members of Parliament quit the government, demanding his resignation. Liz Truss took the role of prime minister on 6 September. Following her resignation on 20 October 2022, she became the shortest-serving prime minister in British history after leading for just six weeks.

People from around the world, fleeing war and other threats to their lives, continued to come to the UK. The Russian government invaded Ukraine, and many British people opened up their homes to refugees.

A new monarch

In 2022, there were street parties and other celebrations for Queen Elizabeth II's platinum jubilee. It marked her 70 years on the throne – the longest reign of any British monarch.

On 8 September 2022, Queen Elizabeth II died at Balmoral Castle in Scotland. There were ten days of national mourning before her state funeral at Westminster Abbey. Huge crowds of people paid their respects along the processional routes and formed a queue that stretched for miles. Her eldest son became King Charles III.

Congratulations!

You have just completed a **whistle-stop tour** through the **history of the lands** that are now called **the UK!**

But there's so much more to find out about the history of the UK and everywhere else in the world. Hopefully, this book has inspired you to find out what interesting stories you can discover in your local area or from your family, friends or the people you live with.

Tragic events often attract the most attention, but don't forget the inspiring and uplifting events you've read about in this book. People might sometimes fight each other, but many have also fought for peace, justice, freedom and a better way of life

Today, we can enjoy longer, healthier lives thanks to clever technologies and improved healthcare. It is exciting to understand how the past affects our lives today, and how we can work together to look after the planet and each other. Who knows what the **future holds** and **how you will affect it?**